In the Footsteps of Francis and Clare

In the Footsteps of
Francis and Clare

Roch Niemier, o.f.m.

Franciscan
MEDIA
Cincinnati, Ohio

Excerpts from *Francis of Assisi: Early Documents*, volumes 1, 2 and 3, edited by Regis J. Armstrong, J.A. Wayne Hellmann and William J. Short, copyright ©1999, reprinted with permission of New City Press. Excerpts from *Francis of Assisi*, by Arnaldo Fortini, copyright ©1992, reprinted with permission of Crossroad Publishing Company. Excerpts from *The First Franciscans and the Gospel*, by Duane Lapanski, copyright ©1976, reprinted with permission of Franciscan Press of Quincy University. Excerpts from *Bread for the Journey: A Daybook of Wisdom and Faith*, by Henri J.M. Nouwen, copyright ©1997, reprinted with permission of HarperCollins Publishers.

Scripture passages have been taken from *New Revised Standard Version Bible*, copyright ©1989 by the Division of Christian Education of the National Council of the Churches of Christ in the U.S.A., and used by permission. All rights reserved.

Photos on pages 7, 15, 28, 34, 49, 55, 66, 72, 77, 83, 88, 98, 104, 108, 113, 121, 127, 137, 143, 147, 154, 166, 176, 185 and 190 by Roch Niemier, O.F.M.
Photos on pages 41, 60, 93, 132, 181 and 195 are courtesy of
Franciscan Pilgrimage Programs.
Photos on pages 1, 22 and 161 courtesy of the Mayo Clinic.

Cover image by Roch Neimier, O.F.M.
Book and cover design by Mark Sullivan

LIBRARY OF CONGRESS CATALOGING-IN-PUBLICATION DATA
Niemier, Roch.
In the footsteps of Francis and Clare / Roch Niemier.
p. cm.
ISBN-13: 978-0-86716-793-1 (pbk. : alk. paper)
ISBN-10: 0-86716-793-9 (pbk. : alk. paper) 1. Francis, of Assisi, Saint, 1182-1226. 2. Clare, of Assisi, Saint, 1194-1253. 3. Spirituality—Catholic Church. I. Title.

BX4700.F6N54 2006
271'.302—dc22

2006028149

ISBN 978-0-86716-793-1

Published by Franciscan Media
28 W. Liberty St.
Cincinnati, OH 45202
www.FranciscanMedia.org

Printed in the United States of America.
Printed on acid-free paper.

[DEDICATION]

This book is gratefully dedicated to the staff of
Franciscan Pilgrimage Programs and all pilgrims who have
journeyed with us throughout the years.

[CONTENTS]

[ACKNOWLEDGMENTS]

I am indebted to Murray Bodo and Joanne Schatzlein for the inspiration and insights they offered at the beginning of this project. In addition, Ramona Miller, Caroline Jakubowski, Joseph Schwab and André Cirino have been invaluable in their critical reading of the text. To all of you, my sincerest thanks. This book is what it is because of you.

I also wish to acknowledge all members, past and present, living and deceased, of the Franciscan Pilgrimage Programs staff, and those who have served in a staff capacity for one pilgrimage or another. Your spirit is reflected in these pages.

[INTRODUCTION]

It seems to me that in certain respects there is not a great difference between the thirteenth and the twenty-first centuries. During the lifetime of Saint Francis there was a burning hunger and desire for things of the spirit, for sound spirituality, for the experience of God. Francis was able to respond to those hungers in a way unmatched, perhaps, by anyone since, and he awakened those hungers in the hearts of others. In our time there is clear evidence of the same kind of desires in people's hearts. They are searching for paths that open them to the realization of their spiritual yearnings.

During the Jubilee Year of 2000 there were many posters on the doors of the major basilicas in Rome with a message from John Paul II. He was speaking to the youth of our time with words of encouragement for young people, telling them not to be afraid of holiness. Perhaps that is what our hearts are seeking: holiness. By holiness I do not mean some pious or otherworldly existence, or a holier-than-thou attitude, but rather a call to a wholesome, genuine and fully committed life based on gospel values. I do not mean something based on legalities or regulations, but on love and compassion that reaches out to people anywhere. This is the source of joy, freedom and the means for promoting the reign of God in our time and rebuilding society, family life and the church.

My personal spiritual journey began in late 1958, the result of a significant religious experience. The presence of God became a very clear reality and a personal relationship with God took hold. I have been blessed, not only with the grace to welcome the relationship, but also to nurture it since that initial moment nearly fifty years ago.

In the process of writing this book I recalled some gifts from those beginning moments. I remembered how in the early months and years that followed I could not get enough of God. There was an almost insatiable desire that manifested itself in various ways: reading, sitting quietly for long periods of time just gazing and wondering about this new awakening, having a feeling of joy and that somehow I discovered a treasure. More importantly, I realized that this desire was something God stirred within me. It was not of my doing. God desired me and wanted me to desire God. This truth has captured and guided my life all these years.

One consequence of the above has been the longing to share with others the wonder of the God I have come to know. This makes me think of the opening words in 1 John:

> We declare to you what was from the beginning, what we have heard, what we have seen with our eyes, what we have looked at and touched with our hands, concerning the word of life—this life was revealed, and we have seen it and testify to it, and declare to you the eternal life that was with the Father and was revealed to us—we declare to you what we have seen and heard so that you also may have fellowship with us; and truly our fellowship is with the Father and with his Son Jesus Christ. We are writing these things so that our joy may be complete. (1:1–4)

I always have had an inner drive to share this wonderful God with others, to let them know what a gracious gift our God is, to tell what I have experienced, what I have tasted, what I have come to know. This longing is ever-present in my spirit. Sometimes it is a roaring fire; other times it is only glowing embers. But the desire has never left me.

contained in a place. First, make an actual visit to the place with the mind-set of a pilgrim. Be open to discovery, receptive to the movement of God's grace; be willing to be changed and to accept a call to holiness.

Second, try to enter into the events of the place as though you were an actor in a drama. We do this at Christmas when we put up a crèche to remind us of Bethlehem, and enter into the mystery of the place by singing with the angels or worshiping the infant with the shepherds. In our Franciscan Pilgrimage Programs, we try to encourage this in a number of ways. We offer lectures to provide the historical context, but we also rely on prayer and Eucharist to help us focus our attention on the same things that Francis and Clare focused on. Some pilgrimage leaders will dramatize Clare's midnight departure from her home and out the Porta Moiano, one of the gates of the city, to join Francis by walking along the path she might have taken and pausing along the way to consider what might have been her thoughts, hopes and fears. Others might ritualize Francis stripping himself before the bishop and his father at Santa Maria Maggiore, standing in that place and reciting the very words Francis spoke at the time. Sometimes we are blessed in the reenactment of Clare's gift of healing in her dormitory at San Damiano where she died. Or at St. John Lateran in Rome we might hear Jesus' call to rebuild the church using stones taken from the Assisi quarry. Other means include the use of music, either songs special to the memory of Francis or suitable to a particular setting or liturgical celebration, the effective use of leisure (spending time at cafés or wandering the streets of Assisi) or by examining the lives of saints.

Third, and perhaps most important, become immersed in the place and its events by reflecting deeply on its meaning for Francis and Clare and also for yourself. Merely going through the motions

This explains the purpose of this book. The pathway i
reflections is among the places that were significant in th
Saints Francis and Clare. They are appealing guides in ou
For the past thirty years I have had the opportunity to lea
groups in central Italy, spending time in Assisi, La Verna,
Valley and Rome, each of these geographical regions prov
setting for significant Franciscan events. A profound sp
has emerged as a result, out of which I draw the reflectio
to share with you.

Permit me, first, to say a word about the spirituality of
Places have their own power, one that evokes meanin
tion and spirit. When we visit them thoughtfully we can ex
the presence of those who have been there before us; we c
something of their spirit. These moments or experien
deeply affect us spiritually. We might have tasted somethin
by visiting the home of a loved one who has recently pass
perhaps in appreciating an experience that would appeal t
one else we know. Marriage counselors often encourage sp
visit the childhood homes of their partners—each learns so
new about the other. At times we might even have exper
strong awareness of the divine presence. This spiritual p
place inspires a unique form of spirituality.

We use this principle to explore the places importan
lives of Saints Francis and Clare because in them we di:
modern-day spirituality that speaks well to our longin;
amazing to visit their city, walk its streets, drink in its spiri
absorbed by the mysticism of every place they touched
lives. Nothing can quite compare with that experience.

As we explore these places together, keep in mind th
important steps to help awaken the spiritual energy

might have some impact, but by choosing to allow ourselves to enter as deeply as possible into the spirituality of a place, we can release the spiritual energy that can draw us deeper into the mystery of God. This is where God touches our lives. This is where we begin to sense the presence of God and some of the hunger within begins to be filled.

Each of the following chapters focuses on a specific place and will offer you the historical context and some suggestions for reflection that you would get on one of our pilgrimages. Whether you are using this book in concert with such a journey, an independent tour or simply as an "armchair" pilgrim, do not cheat yourself by dutifully going from chapter to chapter and place to place without going more deeply. Allow the spirituality of the place to awaken within you a desire for the living God and experience that yearning for holiness being fulfilled in some small way.

Conformity to Christ
San Francesco Piccolino: La Stalletta

Francis of Assisi has often been described as the person in history who most resembled Jesus Christ and gospel living. This idea of Francis' conformity to Christ probably had its beginnings in a work begun in 1385 by Bartholomew of Pisa. He developed highly imaginative stories identifying Francis with Jesus of Nazareth. Each section of his book illustrates some aspect of the life and teaching of the Lord followed by similar material from the life of Saint Francis. Bartholomew called these "conformities."

Bartholomew's work is not alone, though, in noticing these similarities. There are many accounts among Francis' first biographers that talk of his likeness to Christ. Thomas of Celano reminds us, "I consider blessed Francis the holiest *mirror* of the holiness of the Lord, the *image of his* perfection. I think everything about him, both his words and deeds, is fragrant with God's presence."[1]

Before looking at some of these early biographers, it might be helpful to consider briefly a place known as San Francesco Piccolino, or La Stalletta. Many consider it to have been the birthplace of Saint Francis. It is near the main Piazza of Assisi, a short flight of stairs off the Corso Mazzini, or just down a side street next to the Chiesa Nuova (a site claimed by some to be Francis' paternal home). It is a tiny, quiet chapel with a few art pieces that hint at the mystery of birth. The chapel has become a place where local people will pray for the needs of children. Expectant mothers often go there to pray for a healthy pregnancy. The setting invites prayer.

Francis' birthplace is known to us only through legend. No documents or archival papers tell us of the event. Arnaldo Fortini writes:

> According to the legends, Pica, destined to become the mother
> of a saint, came to the end of her term. In astonishment her
> intimate friends and the women of the neighborhood began

to count the days still passing. Yet there was no sign of the expected event. Then, a stranger came to the threshold of the blessed house and gave the young wife the mysterious message that she would not be able to give birth to her baby except in a stable, in the same way that Mary bore Jesus. So Pica was taken to the stable next to the family house. There, on the straw, the baby who would become Saint Francis first saw the light of day.[2]

Don Aldo Brunacci, a respected scholar of Assisi, is certain that La Stalletta is the setting for this legend because of an inscription over the archway that leads into the chapel. The words, printed in Gothic characters, are the earliest information we have and were carved into the stone between 1316 and 1354. They read: *This chapel was a stable, for ox and ass, in which was born Saint Francis, wonder of the world.* A map printed in 1599 also contains a reference to La Stalletta as the birthplace of Saint Francis.

We focus on this place not because of an attractive legend, but because it offers us the opportunity to consider Francis' overall conformity to Christ. The above legend is a gentle starting point. Francis' mother, Lady Pica (his father, Pietro, was away on business in France) could not give birth to her son until she went into the stable connected with the household. As Christ was born in a stable in Bethlehem, so Francis would be born in a stable in Assisi. This speaks to the whole purpose of Francis' life, which was to walk in the footsteps of Jesus Christ as closely as possible.

Aside from this legend, how did the process of becoming like Christ unfold for Francis? Answers come from *The Legend of the Three Companions*, as well as Bonaventure and Thomas of Celano, who were some of the earliest biographers of the saint. They all emphasize that Francis' conformity to Christ began when he encountered Christ while praying in front of the crucifix in the church of San Damiano. As is well known, one day while at prayer in this church, Francis heard Christ speak to him from the cross. Although he would later in life receive the actual wounds of Christ Crucified in his flesh, he nevertheless from that moment carried the wounds of Christ in his heart.[3]

Another important moment came on a February morning in 1208. Francis was attending Mass in the little chapel of the Porziuncola in the valley below Assisi. The Gospel reading that day (Matthew 10:7–14) made so deep an impression on him that, after Mass, he asked the priest to explain it further. Francis immediately acted on what he heard. To be like Jesus, Francis took off his shoes, put down his staff, renounced his wallet and money and threw away his leather belt, crying out, "This is what I want...this is what I desire with all my heart."[4] Bonaventure adds: "He directed all his heart's desire to carry out what he had heard and to *conform* in every way to the rule of right living given to the apostles."[5]

A further example is the story of Francis stripping himself naked before the bishop and his father. Julian of Speyer writes, "Thus he stood completely naked in front of everyone and presented himself as an exile in the world.... Thus the naked man of God had conformed himself to the naked one on the cross, and had perfectly fulfilled the counsel of renouncing all his possessions."[6]

The most telling event that underscores Francis' conformity to Christ is that of the stigmata. Bonaventure describes it well:

> After true love of Christ
> *transformed* the lover *into His image*,
> when the forty days were over that he spent in solitude
> as he had desired,

the angelic man Francis
came down from the mountain,
bearing with him
the likeness of the Crucified,
depicted not on *tablets of stone* or on panels of wood
carved by hand,
but engraved on parts of his flesh
by the finger of the living God. [7]

An equally dramatic moment of Francis' conformity is how he celebrated his own passing by having the brothers bring bread to him, which he blessed and broke and gave a small piece to each of the brothers to eat. This was followed by his having the Passion from John's Gospel read to him.[8] Again Francis was identifying himself with the Lord, consciously leaving his followers a memorial.

After his death one of the brothers had a dream but could not tell if the figure in the dream was Francis or Christ. Celano writes,

> He appeared to him clothed in a purple dalmatic and followed by an innumerable crowd of people. Several separated themselves from the crowd and said to that brother: *"Is this not Christ,* brother?" And he replied: *"It is he."* Others asked him again, saying: "Isn't this Saint Francis?" And the brother likewise replied that it was he. For it really seemed to that brother, and to the whole crowd, as if Christ and Saint Francis were one person.[9]

This is a strong and shocking statement. One might expect the writer to lessen its impact for it is likely that many would be rather skeptical and disturbed about this kind of near-identification of Francis with Christ. Yet Celano does no such thing. Rather he reinforces the impact of the vision because this is what salvation is all about: becoming one spirit with the Lord. And that is what happened to Francis. In his life and mission Francis resembled Jesus Christ himself whose whole life was simply to thrust salvation history and the kingdom forward.

We must be careful, however, not to confuse conformity with external acts. It is true that Francis, with his whole heart, wanted to imitate his Lord and Master. One can easily point to outward similarities, particularly in the way he lived poverty and practiced humility. Yet what is more important is to penetrate Francis' spirit. Above all he wished to conform his heart to Christ, something he realized most clearly in gazing upon the Crucified Savior. In this way Francis sought to take into his heart, into his inner spirit, the poverty, humility and charity so evident in Christ. Conformity for Francis meant a lifelong process of interior transformation. Conformity for Francis meant a heart that was humble. It meant poverty of spirit. It meant a compassion that reached everyone.

His constant concern for the brothers was the same. In his admonitions and exhortations Francis was always admonishing them to purity of heart in all things, to bring their inner spirit in harmony with that of the Lord. That was the only conformity worth pursuing.

What was Francis' goal in this pursuit? To make obvious to a hungry world the kingdom of God. We have no other reason to live.

Pilgrims or visitors to Assisi would do well to search out La Stalletta. This place, where tradition claims Francis' birth was similar to that of Christ's, can touch our heart as we hear our Lord invite us to conform our lives to his. This quiet, out of the way place lends itself to listening well to God's gentle spirit.

Shattered Dreams:
Conversion to Nonviolence
Rocca Maggiore

As a young man Francis enjoyed the same dreams and aspirations of every other young man in Assisi. He wanted to become a knight, to be victorious in battle, to gain glory and wealth and win the hand of a fair maiden. These dreams were shaped, in part, by two experiences. One was the destruction of the Rocca Maggiore by the inhabitants of Assisi in 1198. We can assume that Francis took part in the assault—he would have been sixteen years old at the time. The Rocca Maggiore had been a massive medieval fortress at the top of the hill into which Assisi is built; it had housed the representative of the Holy Roman Empire, which governed and controlled the people in an excessive and heavy-handed way. The destruction of this symbol of oppression brought with it the downfall of feudalism, a way of life that would never rise again. Afterward, the citizens used the rubble to build a wall around the city.

A second formative experience was Assisi's declaration of war against its bitter enemy—the neighboring city of Perugia—in November of 1202. Because of Assisi's success in bringing down the Rocca Maggiore, we can imagine the spirit ignited in Francis. His dreams of knighthood, glory and war were stirred to the depths of his soul. He could feel victory in his bones. He eagerly took up arms to represent his city. The two armies met at Collestrada, about ten miles from Assisi, and the superior forces of Perugia soundly defeated the Assisians. A great many of the defeated soldiers were taken prisoner, among them Francis. His dreams of glory were shattered, and what followed after a year in Perugian prison was a slow shift in his heart. He began to suspect that violence and war were not the path to glory, nor did they solve anything.

The gradual transformation in his spirit began to teach him that violence was not something external to be resisted by setting up walls, or having the finest weaponry to engage in battle or defend possessions. All of these never achieved anything.

Francis learned that the propensity to violence, this inclination to evil in which we all share, is the same motive that keeps alive our judging of others, our greed and anger, our revenge and self-pity, our need to have power and be in control. True violence does not happen outside us; it is the evil in the human heart that is the source of violence. In learning this Francis also learned that the absence of peace, too, is inside the heart, not outside. The only way to peace is to achieve peace of heart, peace of soul, not to take up weapons and engage in war.

Francis gradually embraced this new war. This meant coming to grips with the aggression inside his own heart. The battles were waged in places of solitude. There he came to grips with his own weaknesses—pride, fear, violence, ambition, cowardice and desire for power. He embraced that ominous, negative side of his nature and turned his life over to Jesus to be redeemed. He learned that the person in union with Christ need not fear evil nor deny it. In reliance on Christ and his Spirit the battle with our own violence can be won. What seems bitter and ugly—the recognition of our own capacity for evil—becomes sweet and beautiful when we allow Christ to redeem even what is worst in us.

There is a poignant scene in the movie *Gandhi*. A group of Indians gathered in an enclosed square to listen to someone speak about nonviolence. A British general led troops into the square and blocked any means of escape. He then ordered his men to begin firing. As the killing continued, one of the Indians could be seen running through the crowd and shouting: "Receive their anger; receive their anger." Although a thousand were killed, not one stone was hurled back.

I thought a lot about this (apparently historical) event as I considered nonviolence in my own life. I had been living with someone

who had a volatile, volcanic personality. One day he came screaming at me, frustrated and angry beyond words at something going
on in the community. Being the local minister at the time, he perhaps took it out on me because I happened to be the authority figure. During the outburst I remembered the above scene from the
movie and I kept saying to myself: "Receive his anger; receive his
anger." A deep calm followed, and to this day we share a wonderful
respect for one another.

I experienced something similar during my work with pilgrims
in Italy. Over the years we would go to important sanctuaries, but
often it seemed that the friar caretakers could not care less about
seeing or ministering to another group of pilgrims—perhaps
because they had been too long at the job. They were cranky, angry
and disrespectful. I would say to myself, "Receive their anger; be
kind and respectful." Inevitably there would be a softening in their
demeanor and they would feel good about themselves.

We do not handle violence with violence. Violence is not broken down by becoming violent ourselves, or by returning anger, or
by being offensive to a friar at a sanctuary or a waiter in a restaurant.
We do not handle what is ugly and repulsive with exclusion. We
embrace, we welcome. We offer gentleness. Violence in people's
hearts is broken by nonviolent embrace and forgiveness. Thomas
of Celano relates the following story:

> Once when he was at Colle [Collestrada] in the country of
> Perugia Saint Francis met a poor man whom he had known
> before *in the world*. He asked him: "Brother, how are you
> doing?" The man malevolently began to *heap curses* on his
> lord, who had taken away everything he had. "Thanks to my
> lord, *may the Almighty Lord curse* him, I'm very bad off."
> Blessed Francis felt more pity for the man's soul, rooted in

mortal hatred, than for his body. He said to him: "Brother, forgive your lord for the love of God, so that you may *set your soul free*, and it may be that he will *return* to you *what he has taken*. Otherwise you will *lose* not only your property but also your *soul.*" He replied: "I can't entirely forgive him unless he first gives back what he took." Blessed Francis had a mantle on his back, and said to him: "Here, I'll give you this cloak, and beg you to forgive your lord for the love of *the Lord God*." The man's mood sweetened, and, moved by this kindness, he took the gift and forgave the wrongs.[1]

For Francis, as for us, violence is not something "out there," something external, something to resist with passive techniques. It is not simply shooting or tripping or slugging someone, or pushing someone down the stairs or punching someone in the face, or someone doing those things to us. Violence begins within and is found in the human heart. The absence of peace is also within and therefore must first be found there. Only as our heart begins to be converted are we then able to genuinely take on the conduct of a peacemaker. This does not mean we do nothing in the face of violence. It means we do not respond with the same.

Francis writes in Admonition 13:

Blessed are the peacemakers, for they will be called children of God.
A servant of God cannot know how much patience and humility he has within himself as long as he is content. When the time comes, however, when those who should make him content do the opposite, he has as much patience and humility as he has at that time and no more.[2]

If we claim to be a person of nonviolence and peace, we will know the extent to which we are that person during the moments someone yells and comes at us very angry, or during those moments when we feel cheated and dealt with unjustly. How do we receive such people?

In Admonition 15 Francis adds:

> *Blessed are the peacemakers for they will be called children of God.*
> Those people are truly peacemakers who, regardless of what they suffer in this world, preserve peace of spirit and body out of love of our Lord Jesus Christ.[3]

From the moment of rebirth in the caves near Assisi to the end of his life, Francis responded to violence in himself and others with respect, inclusion and forgiveness.

A key to understanding the spirituality of nonviolence is captured in the words *exclusion versus inclusion*. The stories of the Gospel describe many incidents of the natural tendency to exclude, to keep people at a distance, apart from the in crowd, in other words to maintain a sense of "us versus them," setting up walls and defenses. When, for example, the blind beggar Bartimaeus pleaded for healing from Jesus, the crowd tried to silence and exclude him (Mark 10:46 ff.). As Jesus was dining in the home of a Pharisee, a woman who was a sinner came in. The Pharisee only had disdain for her and considered her an outcast (Luke 7:36 ff.). The same was true for the woman caught in adultery in John 8 and the reaction of the older brother toward the Prodigal Son in Luke 15. Jesus reverses this inclination of the human heart. The outcast, the enemy, the one who is sick in body or spirit, the leper, all are brought into the center of relationship, into the circle of friendship and love. This effected inner peace, healing, forgiveness and would begin the breakdown of violence in people's lives.

If there is anything of which we are certain about Francis, it is that he wanted to imitate his Lord as closely as possible. Forgiveness and peace for Francis meant inclusion. He took as his model the example of Jesus and thus could struggle with the violence in his own life.

We must remember that this is a divine quality. On our own we are helpless. The Lord fills us with his power, a power of love and forgiveness, a power to include. God fills us with his power of reconciling peace because God first does the same to us. God welcomes us into the circle of love, into relationship. With that we are empowered and commissioned to do the same to others.

A fitting conclusion to these comments comes from the Rule of 1223, 3. Francis writes:

> I counsel, admonish and exhort my brothers in the Lord Jesus Christ not to quarrel or argue or judge others when they go about in the world; but let them be meek, peaceful, modest, gentle, and humble, speaking courteously to everyone, as is becoming.... Into whatever house they enter, let them first say: "Peace be to this house!"[4]

Francis practiced what he preached. He was a messenger of peace and nonviolence. His desire for reconciliation with all became the nonviolent charism of Francis of Assisi. Many years ago, Ralph W. Sockman said, "There is nothing as strong as gentleness and nothing so gentle as real strength." How true these words! What courage and conviction of spirit one must have!

The Rocca Maggiore one sees today was rebuilt between the fourteenth and sixteenth centuries. It still towers above the city of

Assisi and reminds one of an imposing imperial fortress from the Middle Ages. It symbolizes the rivalries between pope and emperor, Assisi and Perugia, Maiores and Minores. A pilgrim who visits this stronghold will likely be impressed by its strength and defensive capabilities. It stands forth, however, as a symbol of violence, war and much that defeats the human spirit. It also can serve as a challenge to nonviolence and the pursuit of peace. Perhaps it can give one pause to reflect on Francis' ministry of peace and our call to be peacemakers.

[3]

Francis Meets God
Piazza Comune and Streets of Assisi

The experience of God is an unexpected and totally free gift. It is not we who go in search of God; it is not we who try to make contact with God or pray to God. It always begins the other way around. It is God who desires us, who longs for us. Usually when two persons meet and come to know each other, there are introductions and eventual revelations of one to the other. In the divine economy, however, it is always God who takes the initiative, who comes to meet us.

Francis had several unmistakable moments when this truth bore fruit. One of them took place during his early years on Assisi's streets, or perhaps as he was crossing the Piazza Comune. The *Legend of the Three Companions* tells us:

> A few days after he returned to Assisi, one evening his friends chose him to be in charge so that, according to his whim, he would pay their expenses. He made arrangements for a sumptuous banquet, as he had done so often in the past.
>
> When they left the house bloated, his friends walked ahead of him, singing throughout the city. Holding in his hand the scepter of his office as their leader, he fell slightly behind them. He was not singing, but deeply preoccupied. Suddenly he was visited by the Lord who filled his heart with so much tenderness that he was unable to speak or move. He could only feel and hear this marvelous tenderness; it left him so estranged from any sensation that, as he himself said later, even if he had been completely cut to pieces, he would not have been able to move.[1]

This is a moment of God introducing himself to Francis. It is an overwhelming experience of another capturing his heart. It might be helpful to note that this did not take place in a church, nor while on a retreat or a pilgrimage. It is not even something that Francis pursued or sought out. Rather it took place during a party, a celebration. It was something totally unexpected, a free gift. He did nothing to earn it or make it happen. Perhaps Francis was sitting at one of the outdoor cafes in the piazza, or as the story tells us, while singing along one of the streets leading into the piazza. This is not a fabrication: Every year I still have the experience of young people wandering through the streets of Assisi at night, singing and carrying on as I try to fall asleep.

The account of Francis' encounter with God is crucial. Often people try to discover the one thing that might give them an insight into the heart of Francis. What is the key that unlocks the door to his soul? Francis is perhaps best known for his poverty. He is known as having a universal appeal to people of all backgrounds and religions. He is known as a messenger of nonviolence and peace, as one who loved creation. He is known for his simplicity and humility. Individuals might choose one or another of these facets as that key. Yet not one of them gets to the heart of the question.

The entrance into Francis' heart is his focus on God and his experience of God. God was the center of Francis' world—not brothers and sisters, not making peace, not the poor or the beauty of the created world, not being a gallant and victorious knight or a successful merchant. Francis did, and we can, say yes to all of these, up to a point. But it was the living God who entered his life and made all the difference. This grounded him and he awakened this hunger and the possibility of experiencing God in the hearts of others.

Thaddée Matura writes:

Much is said of Francis' evangelical spirit, its literal application, and his "mimetic" relationship with Jesus and the

Gospels. But one has not understood anything about his adventure as long as one has not grasped how he was a man totally taken up by the desire for God. He lived in a radical way the faith experience, the discovery of God, the mystery of his darkness and light. The cultural and spiritual context of his search was, to be sure, different from ours, but he intuitively understood its primacy, its urgency and its difficulty. The lines in which he speaks of his experience and emphasizes its central place in the Christian life are among the strongest in the spiritual tradition. It is because he was so taken up by his desire for God, even as if drunk with it, that his fidelity to the gospel consisted of an encounter with Jesus, his spirit, more than a rigid and sterile literalism. *Outside of this mooring in the reality of God, which is faith, Francis is unexplainable.*[2]

Certainly one of the most exciting aspects of Saint Francis, as so many of his writings testify, is that he actually met and experienced God in his life and surrendered himself to God completely. The predominance of God in Francis' consciousness is brought home clearly in his *Testament*. He says: The Lord gave me to begin doing penance...the Lord Himself led me among lepers...the Lord gave me such faith in churches...the Lord gave me faith in priests...the Lord gave me some brothers...the Lord revealed to me that I should live according to the pattern of the Gospel...the Lord revealed to me a greeting: *May the Lord give you peace*...the Lord inspired me to write the Rule.[3] This autobiography rings out with the firm conviction it was the Lord who led him every step of the way, and Francis knew it. As he is here reflecting on the stream of his life's journey, he is aware of how God intervened at every major juncture along the way, and his attention is centered on this God.

Or consider his words in the earlier Rule, chapter 23. Francis cannot find enough words to describe the God who has been the God of his life all the way through. He stumbles around looking for whatever words come to his lips. He writes:

> Therefore,
> let nothing hinder us,
> nothing separate us,
> nothing come between us.
> Wherever we are,
> in every place,
> at every hour,
> at every time of the day,
> every day and continually,
> let all of us truly and humbly believe,
> hold in our heart and love,
> honor, adore, serve,
> praise and bless,
> glorify and exalt,
> magnify and give thanks
> to the Most High and Supreme Eternal God
> Trinity and Unity,
> *Father, Son and Holy Spirit,*
> Creator of all,
> Savior of all
> Who believe and hope in Him,
> and love Him, Who,
> without beginning and end,
> is unchangeable, invisible,
> indescribable, ineffable,
> *incomprehensible, unfathomable,*

blessed, praiseworthy,

glorious, exalted,

sublime, most high,

gentle, lovable, delightful,

and totally desirable above all else

for ever.

Amen.[4]

This takes one's breath away.

A careful reading of the early Franciscan sources reveals that the dynamism that powered the life of Saint Francis and that of his followers was provided by the all-good, almighty, eternal and loving God. What the sources stress, and very dramatically so, is that the primitive community enjoyed a very personal and vivid *experience* of God as loving Father. Duane Lapsanski writes, "The fundamental truth about this simple and fascinating man is that at the very core of his being and at the very center of his life, he was filled with God."[5]

I resonate with this description of Francis because when I was nineteen years old, God graced me with a profound religious experience. I had a lot of religion until then, but did not "know" God personally. The initial experience lasted for quite some time and I remember how in the early months and years that followed I could not get enough of God. I can trace the development and growth of that relationship until the present, but God captured my heart and took possession of something inside me.

That is a singular moment in my journey. It has been and always remains the core experience of my life and has grounded me ever since. I define who I am from that point on. It is not my religious vows, or being a priest, or being Catholic, or being a Franciscan, or doing this or that ministry that lays at the foundation of my life. It is rather the conscious awareness of that relationship with God. Sometimes I'd be anxious at the thought that somehow I might do something to "lose" God. The reality, however, is that God will never lose me or leave me, no matter what.

Having said the above I invite you to consider the core religious experience of your life. We all have one, though sometimes it is difficult to name it. What grounds you? What anchors your life?

I think this is what captured Francis. His whole life became a fascination with the Lord, with all of the ups and downs, joys and sins, failures and successes he experienced as a result. His experience of God rooted him. He was firmly convinced that the Lord had touched his life, was leading him, guiding him every step of the way and acting very intimately in his life. This is what he teaches us.

The stories of the early life of Francis, and many others throughout the whole expanse of his journey, verify the fact that it was the experience of God that is the key to unlocking the door to his soul. It is important for the pilgrim who visits Assisi to spend time in the Piazza Comune. While there, sit at one of the outdoor cafés or on the steps leading into the former Temple of Minerva. Order a cappuccino, a glass of beer or a cup of tea and let your imagination run wild. Picture Francis running through this square or along the streets that run in and out of the piazza. Allow your heart to sense God touching you and inviting you to discover your moorings in him alone. This is one way to explore the spirituality of the piazza and streets of Assisi.

Searching for a Rock
The Tomb of St. Peter

People come to Rome, as pilgrims or tourists, for many different reasons. There is history, art, romance, the people, the food, the church, each of which can hold one's attention for days on end. What is a challenge is to discover Francis in Rome, and even more so, specific aspects of spirituality that can touch our lives.

There are three places that make the presence of Francis come alive in Rome: the Tomb of St. Peter, the Basilica of St. John Lateran and San Francesco a Ripa. At these places, as we learn from Franciscan sources, we concentrate on Francis' rooting himself in the faith of the apostles, his relationship to the church and the presence of the poor as seen in the image of the beggar.

From 1202 to 1206, as Francis was trying to figure out his life, he had a need to make a pilgrimage to Rome. His biographers point out that the first thing he did was visit Saint Peter, Prince of the Apostles. *The Legend of the Three Companions* states:

...[H]e yearned to be in another city...as someone unknown....

At this time he happened to go to Rome on pilgrimage. As he was entering the church of Saint Peter, he noticed the meager offerings made by some, and said to himself: "Since the Prince of the Apostles should be greatly honored, why do they make such meager offerings in the church where his body rests?"[1]

Thomas of Celano repeats something similar:

Once on a pilgrimage to Rome, out of love for poverty he took off his fine clothing and dressed himself in a poor man's clothes. He happily settled among the poor in the square in front of the church of Saint Peter....[2]

The Little Flowers of Saint Francis adds the following:

> Saint Francis said [to Brother Masseo], "My dear compan-
> ion, let's go to Saint Peter and Saint Paul, and pray to them
> to teach and help us to possess the immeasurable treasure
> of most holy poverty...[3]

The Basilica, shown in the sketch below, is what Francis knew. This
magnificent but aging Roman structure, however, was dismantled
in 1570 and replaced by the even more spectacular Renaissance
Basilica of St. Peter, which still occupies the spot today.

The Constantinian Basilica of St. Peter[4]

What is important about the basilica then (as now) is that it housed
the Tomb of St. Peter. The remains of Peter that are presently under
the main altar of the current basilica had been in the former
Constantine Basilica. Whether or not Francis prayed before the
actual tomb of Peter as we see it today is unimportant. What we can
say with conviction is that he came to St. Peter's because he
believed that the remains of the prince of the apostles were there,
and he wished to draw inspiration and energy from Peter. Francis
was searching for a foundation, a treasure, a rock on which to set his
whole life and he comes to Peter. Why? Perhaps because Peter is the

first to have made a profession of faith in Jesus Christ. In Matthew 16, Jesus asks his disciples: "Who do you say that I am?" Simon Peter answered, "You are the Messiah, the Son of the living God." And Jesus answered him, "Blessed are you, Simon son of Jonah! For flesh and blood has not revealed this to you, but my Father in heaven. And I tell you, you are Peter, and on this rock I will build my church" (vv. 13–18). Peter proclaims what, and in whom, faith must rest and on whom one's life must be built: the person of the Messiah, the Anointed of God. That witness had to draw Francis to this holy place.

The most important reality in life is the gift of faith in Jesus Christ. That holds everything together and gives one direction and purpose. It is the source of energy for ministry and daily life. It is a source of comfort and consolation on difficult days and often a source of joy and gratitude when awareness comes of what the gift of faith in God has meant. Faith in Jesus is what keeps us going and going and going no matter what. In other words, the foundation of our life is not some structure, or religious laws, or an institution. The foundation of our life is faith in Jesus Christ, a knowledge and relationship with him. Because of that faith we are able to live within structures and institutions and be guided by laws, as was Francis.

What is important is to build moments of faith into our life so that one's foundation becomes deeper and stronger. It usually has to do with stepping into the unknown. The following image might be helpful. Think of being at the edge of a field covered with freshly fallen snow. You need to cross this field but cannot see the well-worn path underneath, cut through the field by many before. Neither can you see the obstacles or shortcuts, because all is covered over. Yet the call of life, the call of love, says, "Come, step out, create new life, new paths." If faith is there, you begin to take one step, then another. All you see is a wide open field and a virgin blanket of snow. And you wonder: What step shall I take? What way is accurate? But you take one step, then another. The key is making the decision to act and taking that first step. Often we talk about "living by faith." We can make plans and discuss our ideas with others. Faith, however, steps in when we decide to take the risk, even before we have solutions and resources to fulfill the plan.

Then after a time on the journey we look back and see our footprints behind us and begin to realize we have been creating the path all along. At the same time we also realize that the Lord has been our guide, and that in his providence God has been watching and caring all the way through. It is, however, a realization or an experience of God we would not have, or come to, unless we took those steps into the unknown to express our trust and faith in God.

These steps into the unknown can take many different forms: asking forgiveness, sharing one's vulnerability, saying to someone, "I love you," accepting a difficult ministry, pursuing a dream or vision that few support or believe in. These are ways we build moments of faith into our life's journey. As this becomes the basis for our life's pattern, our faith becomes firmer, stronger and rock-like. Likewise, the conviction in knowing that God is truly a sure foundation for one's journey in life becomes clear and certain. Others feel and sense this steadiness and firmness in one's spirit that speaks of God.

Francis came to Peter searching for a rock in his life, searching for a foundation. Francis came here to get rooted in the faith of the apostles, which is Jesus Christ. Ultimately, he had only one purpose: to know and experience the living God and awaken that hunger in the hearts of others. All his energy was focused on that goal.

I have several suggestions that might help us do the same, but unless we have very vivid imaginations we may need to get to Rome to carry them out. For example, not far from St. Peter's Square is a street by the name of Via Gregorio VII. A short way up is a bar called Bar Bondolfi. Go there and sit at one of the outdoor tables. Order a cappuccino and look up. Your gaze is easily drawn to the dome of St. Peter's, which rests right over the tomb of Peter. It is as if the faith of that simple fisherman is supporting the entire structure. It is a good symbol.

You can also enter into the magnificent Basilica of St. Peter and take in all the splendor, immensity, art and history. Then think of Saint Paul's words in Philippians 3:8, "I regard everything as loss because of the surpassing value of knowing Christ Jesus my Lord. For his sake I have suffered the loss of all things, and I regard them as rubbish, in order that I may gain Christ." Or visit the tomb of Peter. Ask Peter, as Francis did, to help in discovering the treasure: Jesus the Christ, the Messiah of God.

Beggars, Overcoming Shame
and the Experience of Joy
Basilica of St. Peter

Numerous references in Franciscan sources that speak of Francis' journey to Rome include his experiences with beggars and an effort to understand the meaning of gospel poverty. These moments take place at the Basilica of St. Peter. The three companions make it very clear.

> He [Francis] was so changed by divine grace that, although he was still in secular attire, he yearned to be in another city where, as someone unknown, he would take off his own clothes and, in exchange, put on the rags of a poor man. And he would try begging alms for the love of God.
>
> At this time he happened to go to Rome on pilgrimage....
> [H]e enter[ed] the church of St. Peter....
>
> As he was leaving and passed the doors of the church, where there were many poor people begging alms, he secretly exchanged clothes with one of those poor people and put them on.[1]

Thomas of Celano relates something similar:

> Once on a pilgrimage to Rome, out of love for poverty he took off his fine clothing and dressed himself in a poor man's clothes. He happily settled among the poor in the square in front of the church of Saint Peter, a place where the poor are abundant. Considering himself one of them, he eagerly ate with them. If his embarrassed friends had not restrained him, he would have done this many times.[2]

Francis may have been prepared for such an encounter when on one occasion he met a beggar in his father's cloth shop. He was totally absorbed in the business of selling cloth. Preoccupied with the pursuit of wealth, he paid no attention to a poor man who came in begging alms for the love of God. All of a sudden, as if touched by grace, he realized what he had done and accused himself of great disrespect, especially because the man asked in the name of God. The biographers tell us that he resolved in his heart never again to deny a request to anyone asking in the name of the Most High God.

The experience would serve Francis well on his subsequent pilgrimage to Rome where he encountered beggars at St. Peter's and realized in some lame fashion he was meeting Jesus.

Francis would ask his sisters and brothers to be poor, to become beggars, not because it is such a desirable condition, but because when others meet our poverty we invite them into a moment of conversion. Franciscans are called to challenge people in a dramatic way through their poverty. Franciscans preach by who they are, by confronting another with the poor Christ, so that others are faced with a decision, with a moment of grace. It is true that the poor evangelize us; but even more are we called to evangelize others through our poverty.

In the 1970s and 1980s a group of us friars took up residence in an inner-city area of Milwaukee, Wisconsin. On a corner of our block was a large three-story building that became home for adult men that no one wanted. A man by the name of Larry lived there and took a liking to me. If Larry was outdoors, as I came out of our home, he would run up to me and, with a loud voice and choice language, ask me how I was and how was the pope and the president. And thus we carried on our conversations. Larry, however, took a shower perhaps once every two weeks, rarely shaved, and had a terrible skin condition over his arms, neck and other parts of his body. It got to a point that on leaving the house I would first stick my head out the front door to see if Larry was there. What grew in my awareness, however, was that every time I saw Larry I felt confronted—and certainly challenged—with the gospel. It became clear that my response each time either pointed me toward the gospel, or away from it.

The poor make us face up to the gospel whether we like it or not. We confront this truth over and over again whenever we meet beggars around St. Peter's, or anywhere.

Another way to explore these moments in Francis' life has to do with overcoming shame. This becomes clear when Thomas of Celano's text above is translated: *Many times he would have done a similar thing had he not been held back by shame before those who knew him.* The key phrase is "he would have done a similar thing had he not been held back by shame...". Overcoming shame is something Francis would have to deal with as he encountered new discoveries in his life. The image of the beggar is again helpful for it invites us to look at situations that evoke shame and embarrassment.

In coming to Rome, Francis could get away from home, where people knew him and where he was too embarrassed to act on the stirrings in his heart. In Rome he could join company with new-found friends. Francis was overcoming shame as slowly he developed a confidence to respond to the movements to follow Jesus.

Francis thus consciously put himself in circumstances where he was forced to feel different about himself. The beggar senses this. Usually we're afraid to appear different; we're afraid to appear holy or committed to the gospel. If that controls our responses we can miss many moments when new life and new discoveries are stirring. The beggar image guides us in stepping out of our narrow world into the realm of new possibilities.

So what about shame in our lives? When do we feel it? When we are caught lying? When we mess up a job? When we brag, sound off and later learn we are wrong? In our first sexual experiences? When we carry a secret shame inside that is eating us up because we're too embarrassed to talk about it? When we're ashamed to forgive, be gentle, be holy, let go of revenge?

We can choke off so much life and talents inside because of shame. We can walk through many years with bitterness, a hard heart, no inner peace, because we're ashamed to admit our faults, or talk over our needs, or reveal our genuine self. We often are reluctant to follow Christ well because we are ashamed to live the gospel in front of others. We fear being thought of as different or not a part of the crowd. The image of the beggar is a powerful image. As we deal with the reality of "appearing different," we are invited to overcome shame so that we might be open to all that life offers.

The beggar image speaks deeply to some crucial aspects of our Franciscan charism. For example, the beggar stance implies that we have nothing, that we own nothing and appropriate nothing to ourselves. In other words, the image invites us to approach life with open hands, willing and ready to receive. Likewise, the beggar in each of us gives us the awareness that God alone is the Great Almsgiver. Everything is gift! Everything! As beggars all we can do is open our arms to receive, from which arises the deepest worship we could ever offer our God, namely thanksgiving.

A further insight to all of this comes from Bonaventure's account of Francis' visit to Rome. He writes:

> With religious devotion he visited at this time the shrine of the Apostle Peter. When he saw a large number of the poor before the entrance of the church, led partly by the gentleness of his piety, encouraged partly by the love of poverty, he gave his own clothes to one of the neediest among them. Dressed in his rags, he spent that day in the midst of the poor with an unaccustomed joy of spirit, in order to spurn

worldly glory and to arrive, by ascending in stages, at Gospel perfection.[3]

In his book *Francis of Assisi*, William Cook asks, "What led Francis to this extraordinary act, and why was it a joyful experience?" He surmises, "The joy Francis felt that day may be related to the gratefulness he felt when given even a small coin. Perhaps it occurred to him that everything he had, even his very existence, was a gift. Perhaps there was also a certain brotherhood he discovered with the other beggars that was absent from his own friends in Assisi who enjoyed his life and his largess."[4]

Stand in front of St. Peter's and picture Francis there, exchanging clothes with a beggar and begging himself. He did this to know life more fully and surprisingly he discovered joy. One does not have to become a beggar, but one might try begging, just to see how it feels, just to see what new doors open up inside one's spirit. A pilgrim who goes to Rome might try begging there while away from home where he or she would be unknown. Or it might be enriching to meet a beggar. Look into his or her eyes and offer food or a coin. Try to converse with the person. This could be an excellent way to pick up a sense of the presence and spirit of Francis in Rome. It is a way of entering into the spirituality of the place. Francis did something at St. Peter's that he was ashamed to do in Assisi. He had to get away from his hometown (perhaps we do, too), to discover a new treasure.

The Cross: Discovery of Self and the Rebuilding of Life
San Damiano

Every pilgrim who visits Assisi must make the short walk outside the city walls and spend time at the sanctuary of San Damiano. It is one of the most important in the Franciscan story.

The event most often repeated about this place is the encounter between Francis and the image of Christ crucified who spoke to him and said: "Francis, go rebuild My house; as you see, it is all being destroyed." Thomas of Celano tells the whole story.

> With his heart already completely changed—soon his body was also to be changed—he was walking one day by the church of San Damiano, which was abandoned by everyone and almost in ruins. *Led by the Spirit* he went in to pray and knelt down devoutly before the crucifix. He was shaken by unusual experiences and discovered that he was different from when he had entered. As soon as he had this feeling, there occurred *something unheard of in previous ages:* with the lips of the painting, the image of Christ crucified spoke to him. "Francis," it said, *calling him by name,* "go rebuild My house; as you see, it is all being destroyed." Francis was more than a little stunned, trembling, and stuttering like a man out of his senses. He prepared himself to obey and pulled himself together to carry out the command. He felt this mysterious change in himself, but he could not describe it. So it is better for us to remain silent about it too. From that time on, compassion for the Crucified was impressed into his holy soul. And we honestly believe the wounds of the sacred Passion were impressed deep in his heart, though not yet on his flesh.[1]

Herein begins the mystery of the cross in Francis' life. At first he interpreted his experience in a literal manner, doing all he could to provide the means, with stones and mortar, to rebuild the physical structure of San Damiano that actually was in ruins. Although this may have been part of the intent of the revelation, Francis quickly realized that the rebuilding process had to include the transforma- tion of his heart, his inner self. He would have to rebuild his inner self, and in doing so, discover his true identity. A simultaneous vocation unfolded: rebuilding the place and rebuilding his person.

How did Francis go about rebuilding his life? The process slowly unfolded from his gazing upon the Crucified Savior over time. What were the steps? Saint Clare described it best in her sec- ond letter to Agnes of Prague, when she wrote: "Gaze upon Christ, consider Christ, contemplate Christ, imitate Christ."[2] Those four steps would become the pathway into the discovery of a new heart, a new power and a new self.

The implication and meaning of all of these words will be explored in a later chapter. I want to focus on just the last of these four directives: "imitate Christ." That is the key to understanding what happened to Francis at San Damiano and the key to an effec- tive rebuilding of one's life.

"To imitate" relates to the word "image." In our context here it means I become the image upon whom I gaze. Francis would learn that his self-image, that is, his identity, was to become that of Christ on the cross. Both Francis and Clare must have spent count- less hours contemplating this mystery. The change that would take place within Francis' heart was imaged by what he gazed upon, and this new self would become his tools for renewing the house of God.

The key to this is the Incarnation. In the Incarnation God revealed to us who God is. The Incarnation showed us the face of God. But what does this image portray? What do we see? What Francis and Clare saw in the person of the Incarnate Christ were humility, poverty and charity. The most visible, tangible expression of this was the cross.

In the Incarnation Francis saw that becoming human was the basis for humility. In embracing our humanness Jesus did not cling to being God. This choice was the epitome of humility. In so choosing, Jesus could accept everything to which human nature is prone, even death. This image of Christ as seen on the cross became an essential component of Francis' new self. Like Jesus, humility for Francis meant not to cling to anything or appropriate any goods, titles, honors or position. It meant to be a servant to all, even inanimate things. It meant generosity of spirit and generosity of heart, the willingness to let all others be first. It meant obedience to all, being subject to all, just like Jesus, the Word made flesh, who did not cling to honor, status or power. In recognizing his true self in this image, Francis embraced the essence of his being and that he needed nothing else to give him worth.

The poverty Francis saw in the crucified was the poverty of being a human creature. Although Jesus was God, he did not cling to this status. He didn't hold on to it. In letting go of divinity Jesus accepted the status of a human creature, being dependent, powerless, helpless and empty on his own. This is the essence of poverty. Some call it "poverty of being" or "ontological poverty." This true picture of humanity, modeled in the Incarnation, enabled Saint Paul to write that Jesus, "though he was in the form of God, / did not regard equality with God / as something to be exploited, / but emptied himself, / taking the form of a slave, / being born in human likeness" (Philippians 2:6–7). Jesus, as God, chose to become human, or poor, in order to reveal God's self, which is love, and teach us our true identity. Again this poverty of God was most visible by the fact of God's Son on the cross. Here Jesus embraced powerlessness, emptiness and utter helplessness and opened himself to complete abandonment and trust in his Father.

These were, and are, essential components of the human makeup.

The other element that the image of Christ on the cross portrayed was that of charity—compassionate love. Jesus' outstretched arms drew in all humanity, welcoming every creature into the embrace of God's tender love through mercy, forgiveness and acceptance of all. This meant to recognize and accept the worth and dignity of each one. As we internalize the same we are slowly transformed into the image of Jesus, which is the image of our true self.

The path into this discovery of self is the cross. The cross is a mirror. In seeing myself in that mirror, I see Christ crucified, and in seeing Christ crucified, I see my most authentic self. As I am transformed into that image, I become the person God has always intended me to be. The distinguishing marks that identify me are the same I see in Jesus: poverty, humility and charity, which are identifying marks of the face of God. Paul's words in Galatians 2:20 are then very fitting: "it is no longer I who live, but it is Christ who lives in me." Then I am; I am my true and genuine self.

This reflection is difficult to describe, and I'm sure equally difficult to understand or accept. Yet it lies at the heart of Francis' spirituality and mission. It also ties in most intimately with his experience before the San Damiano crucifix and the invitation to rebuild the church. It was a transformed heart, a transformed self, into the image of Christ that became the tools by which society, the church, and all life could be rebuilt. As we embrace this process, we take a major step toward discovering who we are as disciples of Christ; we are also well on the way to rebuilding our inner life and ultimately rebuilding the house of God.

How can we make this real and concrete? It seems to me we must come to a moment in life where, like Francis, we say: "This is what I *want* and *desire* with all my heart." Once that is clear then the rhythm of daily prayer is essential. We need to beg God for the kind of transformation of heart needed to have a dwelling place for humility and poverty and charity. We cannot achieve this on our own power. It is God's project, God's work, and only grace can make it happen. The other arena is that of relationships, whether among friends, in the family, community life or one's work place. It is here that humility, poverty and compassionate charity are brought to life and nowhere else.

Francis' biographers point out that when people met with Francis, or heard him preach, it was not simply a question of listening to words of peace and joy. Nor were people merely persuaded to reflect upon reasons for forgiving each other, doing penance or thanking and praising God. Rather, they were confronted with these realities in the person of Francis. They were in the living presence of forgiveness, peace, faith and love, because Francis had integrated these values into his person by taking on the image of Christ on the cross. Francis became conformed to the Crucified to such a degree that at the end of his life he appeared like the Crucified with the wounds of Christ engraved into his flesh. This would complete what began at San Damiano when the wounds of the sacred Passion were impressed deep in his heart, though not yet on his flesh.

Francis sought repeatedly for ways to encourage the brothers to give birth to these essentials, to strive for purity of heart, and thus give birth to Christ in their own lives. This is the transformation that must go hand in hand with all other endeavors in proclaiming the kingdom of God. This is the inner rebuilding that gives life and spirit to any outward effort.

The image of Christ in Francis was very real as we read in Celano:

The brothers who lived with him know

that daily, constantly, talk of Jesus was always on his lips,

sweet and pleasant conversations about Him,

kind words full of love.

Out of the fullness of his heart his mouth spoke.

So the spring of radiant love

that filled his heart within

gushed forth.

He was always with Jesus:

Jesus in his heart,

Jesus in his mouth,

Jesus in his ears,

Jesus in his eyes,

Jesus in his hands,

he bore Jesus always in his whole body....

With amazing love he bore

in his heart and always held onto

Christ Jesus and Him crucified.[3]

A pilgrimage to Assisi would be incomplete without time at the sanctuary of San Damiano. This place is most quiet and suitable for prayer in the early morning, before ten o'clock, or in the early evening. Sit before the crucifix, listen to your heart and hear Jesus say: "Jim, Joanne, David, Beth, Jerry, Bob, Susie, Carol, go, rebuild my house; as you see, it is all being destroyed." Or visit the Basilica of Saint Clare within the walls of Assisi. The original crucifix of San Damiano is housed there. It is unmistakably a place of prayer where the windows of one's heart may open to hear the voice of God. In the cross the pilgrim discovers his or her true identity and finds the rebuilding tools needed to renew the house of God.

[7]

The Wisdom of Solitude
Carceri

The experience of solitude is not easy to deal with. Not much in human nature finds it attractive. Our cultural patterns of constant activity work against it. Yet the nurturing of this contemplative dimension of life is so important that without it something essential is missing from wholesome human life and from the totality of a Franciscan vocation.

The early sources are unanimous in reporting that going off to places of solitude held a great attraction for Francis. Even before his conversion we see Francis drawing away from his carefree companions and retreating to some solitary place, such as the caves near Assisi. There he prayed and begged the Lord for light. Such prayer in solitary places became characteristic of Francis' life and remained so to the very end.

Celano, among others, testifies to the truth of this practice.

> For his safest haven was prayer;
> not prayer of a fleeting moment, empty and proud,
> but prayer that was prolonged,
> full of devotion, peaceful in humility.
> If he began at night,
> he was barely finished at morning.
> Walking, sitting, eating, drinking,
> he was focused on prayer.
> He would spend the night alone praying
> in abandoned churches and in deserted places
> where,
> with the protection of divine grace,
> he overcame his soul's many fears and anxieties.[1]

The personal practice of Francis going off to isolated spots for periods of time in order to give himself to serious prayer left its mark not only on the memory of his biographers, but also on the visible landscape of the Italian countryside. Even today many can see for themselves where Francis spent hours and days in prayer, places like Montecassale, La Verna, Celle di Cortona, Speco di Narni, Fonte Colombo, Poggio Bustone, Bellegra, to name a few. Another place was the Carceri, located outside Assisi on Mount Subasio. In other words, Francis didn't meet God in a haphazard way. He sought out places of quiet; he took pains to go away. He went up the mountain, out to an island, into a church, at the beginning of night or early morning. It took no small effort to reach any of these places, which were purposely chosen for their out-of-the-way character.

As Christ was Francis' example of service to others, he was also his example and inspiration for going off to lonely places. The amount of time Jesus took for his apostolic solitudes is amazing when we consider who he was and his relationship with his Father. The Gospels report the following:

But now more than ever the word about Jesus spread abroad; many crowds would gather to hear him and to be cured of their diseases. But he would withdraw to deserted places and pray. (Luke 5:15–16)

Now during those days he went out to the mountain to pray; and he spent the night in prayer to God. (Luke 6:12)

That evening, at sundown, they brought to him all who were sick or possessed with demons. And the whole city was gathered around the door.... In the morning, while it was still very dark, he got up and went out to a deserted place, and there he prayed. (Mark 1:32–35)

Immediately he made his disciples get into the boat and go on ahead to the other side, to Bethsaida, while he dismissed

the crowd. After saying farewell to them, he went up on the
mountain to pray (Mark 6:45–46).

Our Lord took pains to provide for solitude. He simply didn't let
these moments happen, nor did he take time only when he felt like
it. It's an example for us who are busy, sometimes beyond imagination, that periods of time alone with God are indispensable for
union, for coming to experience God. The example of Christ was
also an example for Francis.

Why did Francis build this rhythm into his life? Answering
this question opens a door to what one might call "the wisdom of
solitude."

First and foremost, solitude offers an opportunity for self-
knowledge in a way that no other experience can provide. I have
the chance to expose my human nature to myself in the raw and see
how I truly am next to God. In solitude I get rid of my scaffolding:
no friends to talk with, no telephone calls to make, no meetings to
attend, no music to entertain, no books to distract, no prayers to
say. Just me: naked, vulnerable, weak, sinful, broken. It is this
powerlessness, this poverty, this nothingness that I have to face in
my solitude, something so difficult that everything in me wants to
run to my friends, my work, my distractions, so that I can forget
this and make myself believe I am someone important or something else.

Thomas of Celano underscores this truth admirably when he
writes:

...leaving public places
he [Francis] sought places of solitude,
where he was often instructed by visits of the Holy Spirit....
As he began to visit hidden places conducive to prayer, the

devil struggled to drive him away with an old trick. He made Francis think of a horribly hunchbacked woman who lived in town and whose looks scared everyone. The devil threatened that he would become like her if he did not turn back sensibly from what he had begun. But, *strengthened by the Lord*, he rejoiced at a response of healing and grace....[2]

From 1971 to 1974 I was working with our college formation program in Milwaukee, Wisconsin. The afternoon hours were the best time for prayer when the house quieted down. I usually tried to spend about an hour in a relaxed contemplative setting. For three years, almost daily, the first fifty to fifty-five minutes of that hour were sheer hell, filled with distractions, questions about the students and concerns of all sorts. Natural instinct would say that it was all a waste of time—useless. Even the laziest person finds himself thinking, "Let me do something *productive*." I knew by then, however, the importance of staying with it. And nearly every day during the final five minutes a peaceful calm took over, filled with insight, wisdom and a sense of direction.

What I learned was that the whole process taken together constitutes the prayer-solitude dynamic. The final five minutes issued in an experience of God that I would have missed completely had I not stayed there. I have learned since to trust the movement of God's Spirit within my spirit coming out of such prayer. Now when such moments come, I have confidence that it is God's presence and Spirit at work in me.

As one has the courage to become comfortable with oneself, which happens in the experience of solitude, self-discovery emerges with the potential for growth in inner freedom and integrity of life. New insights become known, a deeper self-confidence arises, all due to insightful self-knowledge.

Henri Nouwen reminds us that whether solitude is connected with a physical space or not, it is essential for our spiritual lives.

> It is not an easy place to be, since we are so insecure and fearful that we are easily distracted by whatever promises immediate satisfaction. Solitude is not immediately satisfying, because in solitude we meet our demons, our addictions, our feelings of lust and anger, and our immense need for recognition and approval. But if we do not run away, we will meet there also the One who says: "Do not be afraid. I am with you, and I will guide you through the valley of darkness."[3]

In quiet we also put ourselves into the context for meeting the transforming power of Christ, and the realization that he alone can remake our hearts into his image. In other words, solitude gives one the opportunity to surrender to Christ and experience rebirth as Francis did in the caves around Assisi.

One does not go into solitude just to be there, or to be alone, or to struggle with one's false self or demons. That would be sadism. A person builds a rhythm of solitude into life because of a need to meet and surrender to Christ. One may resist that, but it is a need. It is not possible to maintain and nurture a life of solitude without this dynamic. I must be aware that I want to meet Christ in my solitude. The surrender may be just for a moment, but if it is unconditional at that moment, there is peace and calm. We know the nearness of the Lord and then it is possible to encounter the transforming power of our God.

Further, solitude builds fraternity. It is no accident that in Francis' *Rule for Religious Life in Hermitages* he insists that the setting always includes three or four brothers together. Fraternity is all about solitude greeting solitude. It is not the place where we are no longer alone but the place where we respect, protect and greet one another's aloneness. Nouwen writes: "Our solitude roots us in our own hearts. Instead of making us yearn for company that will offer us immediate satisfaction, solitude makes us claim our centre and empowers us to call others to claim theirs. Our various solitudes are like strong, straight pillars that hold up the roof of our communal house."[4]

Each of us is unique. The practice of solitude uncovers and heightens that uniqueness, and fraternal life deepens in the respect and support the brothers give to each one's unique aloneness. This was Francis' genius as he arranged for life together in a solitude setting. One can visit any number of hermitages in central Italy that preserve individual caves, or grottoes, that the brothers used. Always included were arrangements for the brothers to come together for specific times of the day. These were, and still are, some of the warmest centers of hospitality and life together as brothers.

Most importantly, however, we build a rhythm of daily solitude into life in order to clarify and reaffirm the primacy of God. God alone is God and no other. Daily life tends to turn us away from such awareness with its concerns and chaotic busyness. The rhythm of regular prayer in solitude turns us back to it. It gives us the opportunity to reaffirm again that God is, and only God. As time passes, that truth deepens within one's heart. It keeps a sustained focus on God and slowly develops a rhythm of interior continuity that solidifies that perspective with deeper and deeper conviction.

Of all the sanctuaries in and around Assisi, no other place has such natural beauty as the Carceri. The pilgrim who explores the sanctuary will discover Leo's grotto and those of Masseo and

Rufino. Their names are written over their personal caves. These
three are on the side of the mountain. Francis' grotto is preserved
within the main structure of the sanctuary.

Francis and the first brothers developed a new life, a new out-
look, a new society, and worked at it. They sought to "seek first the
Kingdom of God and his justice." What gave the movement impetus
came from the example and encouragement of Francis and from
regular meetings when the brothers shared and strengthened one
another. All of this, however, was brought to fruition in the practice
and experience of solitude. One cannot understand the early movement's success without this dimension from which the Franciscan
movement established itself for all time.

8

Meeting and Embracing a Leper
La Maddalena

Francis writes in his *Testament*:

> The Lord gave me, Brother Francis, thus to begin doing penance in this way: for when I was in sin, it seemed too bitter for me to see lepers. And the Lord Himself led me among them and I *showed mercy* to them. And when I left them, what had seemed bitter to me was turned into sweetness of soul and body.[1]

"When I was in sin," didn't necessarily mean performing sinful actions. It included the setting up of other gods or idols in Francis' heart such as money, pleasure, ambition, fame or power. It wasn't that these were bad. It was simply a heart in the wrong direction. The Lord then gave Francis the ability to "do penance" by visiting and serving lepers. "To begin to do penance," again did not refer to specific acts of mortification, but referred to the turning of one's heart to Christ and the gospel. It was that grace of freedom from the idol of self-centeredness coupled with the gift of the most wonderful of all discoveries: that one's only true center is God and any grounding other than God is a false grounding.

If penance means to break with the past that is precisely what happened to Francis in his experience with the leper. The kiss with this unfortunate person brought about a deeper realization of the source of his happiness and true identity. In embracing the leper Francis began to embrace his true self.

There were several hospitals for lepers in the Assisi region during the time of Saint Francis, but the one that played a large role in the life of Francis was called San Lazzaro of Arce, later renamed Santa Maria Maddalena. Tradition tells us there were two chapels on this property. One was named San Rufino d'Arce (not the same as the Cathedral of San Rufino in Assisi) and served the needs of the male lepers. The other was called Maria Maddalena and cared for the spiritual needs of the women. Some would claim that San Rufino d'Arce served lepers who were poor while Maddalena catered to those who came from a wealthy background. La Maddalena remains a place of prayer and devotion for the local residents of the area. San Rufino d'Arce is now cared for by Franciscan sisters who live in a convent connected with this chapel. Both chapels still exist in the valley below Assisi. They lie about halfway between San Damiano and the Porziuncola.

A road in the Umbrian valley connects the village of Saint Mary of the Angels and the city of Foligno. Along that road lies the Maddalena chapel. At that juncture traffic can be life threatening if one is not careful. Nearby there is a spur that cuts off from this main road and takes one toward Assisi. It is probable that on this road Francis met the leper as described in *The Legend of the Three Companions*:

> One day he was riding his horse near Assisi, when he met a leper. And, even though he usually shuddered at lepers, he made himself dismount, and gave him a coin, kissing his hand as he did so. After he accepted a kiss of peace from him, Francis remounted and continued on his way. He then began to consider himself less and less, until, by God's grace, he came to complete victory over himself.[2]

Bonaventure adds that after touching and kissing the leper and remounting his horse, Francis turned around, looking in all directions onto an open plain. But the leper was nowhere to be seen.

In Mark 1:40–42, Jesus cures a leper in the gesture of touching him. At first glance, this story seems to be one more of the many cures that Jesus performed in his public ministry. But on a deeper level, it deals with the social exclusion of the sick. Jesus' culture would have thought Jesus leprous as well after he touched the man who had leprosy. The Gospel writer is clear, "Jesus stretched out his hand and *touched* him" (emphasis added). Jesus was willing to suffer the social consequences of the touch.

Francis was willing to suffer the same social consequence when he decided to dismount, touch and kiss the leper, and even more so to live among them. Little by little his social identity and relationships changed and provided surprising new awareness of himself. A similar realization is described in the following story.

Some years ago Bishop Fulton Sheen had a prime-time TV show opposite Milton Berle every Wednesday night. One night he told about his visit to an African leper colony. He had brought along a supply of little silver crucifixes so he'd have something special to give to each of the five hundred lepers in the camp. The first leper he met had only the stump of his left arm. And his right arm and hand were covered with ugly, open sores. Sheen took one of the little crucifixes, held it a few inches above the leper's hand, and then let it drop into his palm.

In a flash he was struck by what he had done. "All at once," he said, "I realized there were 501 lepers in the camp, and the most leprous of them all was myself. I'd given a crucifix—the symbol of God's absolute love for us all—but then I'd pulled back and closed my eyes to what that symbol implied for me. So I looked again very hard at that little crucifix, and I knew what I had to do. I pressed my hand to the leper's hand with the symbol of love between us, and then I proceeded to do that for all of the remaining 499 lepers."

The embrace of the leper illustrates so well the process of embracing fear that is so often the root of violence, defensiveness and the exclusion of others. This experience is symbolic of embracing something inside ourselves that we do not like: crabbiness, anger, meanness, greed, selfishness. When we are unable to accept any of these, we usually project these qualities onto others; we keep them at a distance; we see them as the enemy out to get us. This moment shows how Francis came to be reconciled with fear, with what is repulsive, ugly and dirty. It was a clear example of the old self being deconstructed and the new self being built.

The embrace of the leper was a major uncovering moment in Francis' conversion journey. In that encounter something shifted radically inside his heart and transformed his vision of reality. This was the turning in his heart that would make all the difference and this turning was now set in motion. In addition Francis felt a new power within for shortly afterward Francis began to live among the lepers. He began to "show mercy." Some would translate these words to read, "he would practice mercy toward them." And once Francis got past this experience, and knew deep in his being what it meant to practice and offer mercy, it was a logical step for him to begin reaching out in a similar manner to everyone: robbers, the poor, Saracens, the arrogant, the powerful. All were deserving of respect, honor, inclusion and acceptance. Each one had worth and he was empowered to acknowledge and affirm that.

Most of us are not lepers. But there's not one of us whose heart has not been wounded or even broken many times. There's not one of us who doesn't need healing. So it is to all of us that Jesus and Francis speak by their actions. In stretching out his hand, touching that leper and healing him, in getting off one's high horse and allowing compassion to surge within one's heart, we learn that God does love us no matter how damaged or broken we are and offers us healing.

But in addition to what God wants to do for us, there's the matter of what God wants us to do for one another. We too are to be healers, to reach out and touch the marginal, the outcast, to bring respect and dignity into others' lives. Like Francis we will never be able to let go of this vision.

What was awakened in Francis was the *capacity for mercy*. In our own struggle to shift from a focus on self to the misery of another person is perhaps the lesson and inspiration we receive from the spirituality of this place. In awakening the capacity for mercy, it was also the leper who set the seal of Christ in Francis' innermost being. That was Francis' moment of conception that would grow into the birthing of Christ for all the world to see.

Some scholars in Assisi believe in the likelihood that in the early days of the Franciscan story, before Clare and her sisters were fully cloistered, Francis and the brothers would come from the Porziuncola to minister to the lepers, and Clare and her sisters would come from San Damiano to do the same. The leper colony was a short walking distance from either of the two places.

If blessed with an opportunity to visit La Maddalena in the valley below Assisi, ask the woman who lives in the house next to this wayside chapel for the key. Enter this seldom-used holy place, imagine the lives who passed through its doors. Feel the walls, hear their cries and welcome the presence of Christ who invites us to a conversion of heart, who invites us to break down walls that keep anyone outside. Let your spirit and heart be moved, as was Francis', to practice mercy and compassion.

9

Undressing One's Heart to the World
Santa Maria Maggiore

The one event that happened at Santa Maria Maggiore (the former cathedral and bishop's residence in Assisi), for which Francis is remembered, is his stripping himself naked before the bishop, his father Pietro and the local citizens of Assisi. It was another telling moment in his conversion journey. We know Francis' father was irate beyond words. His son, unintentionally, was making a mockery of him, was an embarrassment to the family and stole some merchandise from his cloth shop. Pietro was fed up with Francis and tried to summon him before the civil authorities. When that didn't work he appealed to the bishop whose residence was at Santa Maria Maggiore. *The Legend of the Three Companions* picks up the story:

> Then he came before the bishop and was received by him with great joy. "Your father," the bishop said to him, "is infuriated and extremely scandalized. If you wish to serve God, return to him the money you have, because God does not want you to spend money unjustly acquired on the work of the church. [Your father's] anger will abate when he gets the money back. My son, have confidence in the Lord and act courageously. Do not be afraid, for He will be your help and will abundantly provide you with whatever is necessary for the work of his church."
>
> Then the man of God got up, joyful and comforted by the bishop's words, and, as he brought the money to him, he said, "My Lord, I will gladly give back not only the money acquired from his things, but even all my clothes." And going into one of the bishop's rooms, he took off all his clothes, and, putting the money on top of them, came out naked before the bishop, his father, and all the bystanders, and said, "Listen to me, all of you, and understand. Until

now I have called Pietro di Bernadone my father. But, because I have proposed to serve God, I return to him the money on account of which he was so upset, and also all the clothing which is his, wanting to say from now on: 'Our Father who are in heaven,' and not 'My father, Pietro di Bernadone.'"[1]

One of the ways to explore the spirituality of this event has to do with intimacy. Nakedness has overtones of intimacy, which is each person's deepest need. In using the word "intimacy," the intent is the sharing of one's heart, one's deepest self. The reference is not to sexual activity, but to the bonding of spirit and life that goes on in genuine relationships. Everyone wants and longs for someone with whom to uncover one's heart.

When intimacy happens, it affects every aspect of life in a way nothing else can: ministry, work, family, community, faith life, one's image of God and one's personal self-image. In other words, our experience of intimacy affects the way we pray, the way we minister, the way we forgive, the way we live, the way we relate to our spouses, sisters and brothers, the way we hope and the way we dream about our future.

Likewise, when intimacy happens, all kinds of energy are released: for good, for creativity, for enthusiasm, for fidelity, for artistic expression, for relationships, for the giving of oneself to commitments, the vows, the gospel, for coming to know God.

Professor Barta at Loras College in Dubuque, Iowa, once made the comment, "The most profound moment in life is the moment when you realize that someone with whom you would like to be intimate, would like to be intimate with you." He paused, then repeated the statement. "Then," he continued, "you could walk for forty days and forty nights on the energy that is released."

The path for movement into intimacy is the uncovering of the self or the undressing of the heart, a form of nakedness. Intimacy requires what we call psychological nakedness. Psychological nakedness, someone has said, is an undressed heart. Every human being longs for that gift. Undressing one's body with another is one thing. Undressing one's heart, however, is quite something else.

Jesus undressed his heart before his disciples, revealing to them everything of God and all the mysteries of the kingdom. Francis' gesture of undressing his body was a symbolic gesture in the ongoing process of undressing his heart to the world, which to this day attracts us to him and the gospel.

I have two very intimate friends. One of them is a friar whom I have known for more than forty-five years. The other is a woman, a fellow religious, whom I have known for more than thirty-five years. Over the years we have shared much at just about every level of life one can imagine. I have never had to undress my body with them, but I have undressed my heart, and they have done the same.

The "undressing of hearts" is really the heart of the matter. Every time this takes place, whether in the bonding of a very close significant friend or as brothers or sisters who love and support each other in a local fraternity, or between husband and wife, all kinds of energy are released. Faith is enhanced, life happens, ministry is strengthened, joy is felt, healing takes place. We feel a surge of hope, a spirit of creativity opens up and our vision of Franciscan and gospel life gets clearer.

In the book *St. Francis and the Foolishness of God*, the authors write:

> The more deeply we experience intimacy with another person, the more likely we are to be open to the love of God. Jesus and the Magdalene, Francis and Clare did this. We

simply have to put aside all of the fears and second thoughts that the offer of intimacy brings. Despite the acknowledged risks that relationships carry with them, they are from God. They have been entered into by the Clares and Francises of history and they are the one surest safeguard from the sterile individualism that so afflicts modern society.

There are important links between intimacy and spirituality, between life in God and life in another. Life in God, for example, requires an other-centeredness not unlike selfless friendship. Life in God requires that we move our centers of gravity outside of ourselves to dance the dance of life with all peoples and all of creation. Intimate friendship calls us to dance that dance with the other as well. Life in God requires that we risk all in the cosmic effort to live justly. Intimacy requires that we risk as well—in the miraculous discovery of mutually respectful, life-giving, and just relationships.[2]

When Francis stripped himself naked at Santa Maria Maggiore, he was reaching for the heart of God. The undressing of his body was merely a symbolic gesture of the undressing of his heart. Most or all of us will never have reason to do what Francis did. Perhaps, though, we can hear in this holy place the call to have the courage to undress our hearts with another and to deepen that grand mystery of intimacy that leads us into the tender heart of God and the wonder of life with him.

The Word! The Word! The Word!
Porziuncola

In his *Testament* Francis wrote, "The Most High revealed to me that I should live according to the Holy Gospel." Francis is convinced of this truth because of the undeniable intervention by the Lord that happened on February 24, 1208, at the Porziuncola. This tiny chapel was, and still is, located in the Umbrian valley about two miles from the city of Assisi. While at Mass he heard the Gospel in a way never before experienced by him. As the celebrant read the text, the words went directly to Francis' heart. They rang out clearly and distinctly in the quiet solitude of that little church. The passage may have been from Matthew, Mark or Luke. This is Matthew's account:

> [Jesus said,] "As you go, proclaim the good news, 'The king-dom of heaven has come near.' Cure the sick, raise the dead, cleanse the lepers, cast out demons. You received without payment; give without payment. Take no gold, or silver, or copper in your belts, no bag for your journey, or two tunics, or sandals, or a staff; for laborers deserve their food. Whatever town or village you enter, find out who in it is worthy, and stay there until you leave. As you enter the house, greet it. If the house is worthy, let your peace come upon it; but if it is not worthy, let your peace return to you. If anyone will not welcome you or listen to your words, shake off the dust from your feet as you leave that house or town." (Matthew 10:7–14)

This was a pivotal moment in Francis' conversion itinerary. All the narratives relate that in this proclamation of the Gospel, Francis was so struck by it that his everyday life was turned upside down. Celano, Bonaventure and the three companions make of the scene a decisive turning point in Francis' life. It is helpful to remember that he had already experienced the message from the San Damiano crucifix; he encountered the leper and kissed him; he had stripped himself before the bishop and his father; but the direction for his life's journey was still unclear. All now came together upon hearing the Gospel that day. At last Francis had found his vocation. Celano tells it well:

> One day the gospel was being read in that church about how the Lord sent out his disciples to preach. The holy man of God, who was attending there, in order to understand better the words of the gospel, humbly begged the priest after celebrating the solemnities of the Mass to explain the gospel to him. The priest explained it all to him thoroughly line by line. When he heard that Christ's disciples should not *possess gold* or *silver* or *money*, or *carry on their journey a wallet or a sack*, *nor bread nor a staff*, nor *to have shoes* nor *two tunics*, but that they should preach *the kingdom of God* and *penance*, the holy man, Francis, immediately *exulted* in the *spirit of God*. "This is what I want," he said, "this is what I seek, this is what I desire with all my heart."[1]

These words strikingly indicate that Francis was totally present to this moment of inspiration, listening carefully to what the Lord was saying to him. Filled with joy he plunged into fulfilling the gospel message. Acting from the very depths of his being, Francis finally knew what he wanted and followed his heart. The revelation that came from this Gospel text opened up to him a radically new way of life. Thus he could say, "No one showed me what I was to do, but God revealed to me that I should follow the way of the Gospel." Duane Lapsanski writes:

> In his writings the saint described this life which he and his brothers began to observe at God's inspiration: they sold all

their possessions and gave to the poor; they were content with a single tunic, cord and trousers; they stayed in churches, were unlearned and subject to all. Faithful to the advice Christ gave to his apostles, the brothers carried nothing on their journeys, used the salutation of peace, and ate and drank what was set before them. They did not contend in words, but were at peace with each other. They shared their goods with all who asked of them and preached to people by word and example, admonishing them to turn their hearts to the Lord. Finally, they fasted, prayed and worked with their hands.[2]

What did this experience of hearing the Word do? The impact of the Word was so strong that when Francis' first companion, Bernard, asked to join him, he went back to the Word. Joined by Peter Catanio they went to the Church of San Nicolo and consulted the Gospel three times to find out what their way of life ought to be. Having found the same set of requirements for discipleship (see Matthew 19:21; Luke 9:3; Matthew 16:24), Francis said, "Brothers, this is our life and rule and that of all who will want to join our company. Go, therefore, and fulfill what you have heard."[3]

When his companions numbered eleven, Francis prepared a Rule of Life based on the Scriptures to present to Pope Innocent III for confirmation. Again this stemmed from his Porziuncola experience. When Clare joined the movement, Francis prepared a Rule of Life for her and her sisters, again based on Scripture texts. And he would go to the same source when the laity, the Seculars, asked him for a way of life.

Likewise, we know that when Francis was invited to preach at the Cathedral of San Rufino, he would prepare the whole night to announce and proclaim the Word.

Often throughout his life Francis would simply consult "The Book." For example, when in 1221 the Non-Confirmed Rule was prepared, the text consisted almost entirely of Scripture passages.

One time a certain brother saw Francis in great pain and encouraged him to seek consolation in the written Word of God. Francis' response to this suggestion was, "It is good to read the testimonies of Scripture, and it is good to seek the Lord our God in them. But I have already taken in so much of Scripture that I have more than enough for meditating and reflecting. I do not need more, son; *I know Christ*, poor and *crucified*."[4]

Beginning with this February morning Francis was no longer a deaf hearer of the Gospel, but he now put into his good memory everything he heard. Francis was convinced that the Gospel life he adopted stemmed from that undeniable intervention of the Lord on February 24, 1208. He would spend his life on the road living and proclaiming that Gospel.

I think this is the key event linked with St. Mary of the Angels, the Porziuncola. The Gospel, the Word of God, became the core of existence for Francis. The Gospel directed his form of life, animated his relationships. The Gospel energized and gave form to his activity and ministry. The Gospel constituted the very marrow of life of the brothers, the Poor Ladies (Poor Clares), and the laity interested in following him. This Holy Book was for him a Person—living. This Book was at the beginning of Francis' new life in 1208. This Book was present at his final moments.

Between these two Gospel proclamations—hearing the Gospel in February 1208 and having it read to him as he lay dying in October 1226, an entire personal and communal experience unfolded out of which Francis faced up to the demands of the Book. He went out on the road and proclaimed good news. He proclaimed like a poor person. He announced peace and forgiveness as a constant. He called others to conversion of heart and he announced the arrival of the kingdom, the reign of God.

Every pilgrim who comes to Assisi must spend time at the Porziuncola. Take along a book of the Gospels, feel the stones in the walls, call upon God's blessing, sit in silence and allow the spirit of the Word to enter in and renew your life.

First Brother
Bernard of Quintavalle

HIC
S. FRANCISCVM
AD CŒNAM, ET CVBITVM
B. BERNARDVS QVINTAVALLIS
EXCEPIT ET
IN EXTASIM VIDIT.

Francis' changed life began to be noticed in Assisi. Some young men were so moved that, like Francis, they felt inspired to leave all things behind and join him. The first of these was a highly respected man by the name of Bernard of Quintavalle. Bernard was respected not only for his nobility and wealth, but above all for his learning. He was puzzled by the change in Francis, unable to understand what was taking place. Francis' humility, firmness of purpose, joy of spirit, somehow gave Bernard the feeling that Francis had discovered a hidden treasure. So Bernard decided to look into the matter.

One evening he invited Francis to his home. It was probably early April of 1209. They sat down to dinner and Francis talked passionately of the new life he discovered in the Gospel, with all of his dreams and ideals coming alive in the service of a new Lord, Jesus Christ, and his kingdom.

Listening and watching with penetrating eyes, Bernard felt his heart opening. For a first time he caught a vision of a new kind of world, and his previous life suddenly seemed an abyss—empty, dark and meaningless. He considered this with astonishment.

Francis spent the whole night with him. Afterward Bernard said to him:

"If, for many years, someone holds on to the possessions, many or few, he has acquired from his lord, and no longer wishes to keep them, what is the better thing for him to do with them?" Blessed Francis answered that he must give back to the lord what was received from him. And Lord Bernard said: "Then, brother, I want to give away all my worldly goods for the love of my Lord who gave them to me, as it seems best to you." The saint told him: "We will go to the church early in the morning and, through the book of the Gospels, we will learn how the Lord instructed his disciples."[1]

Bernard experienced a passionate desire for something other than what life had given him. Like him, our desires are the deepest cravings of the heart. Bonaventure claims that God infuses desires within us and draws us in a hidden way to him. After Francis heard the Gospel at the Porziuncola on February 24, 1209, and understood what it asked, he cried out, "This is what I *desire with all my heart*."[2] After Bernard spent the night conversing with Francis, he could no longer contain himself and exclaimed, "I want to give away all my worldly goods for the love of my Lord who gave them to me."[3] This movement is God's doing, not one's own. We experience a longing for God, but *it comes out of God's longing for us. God desires us.*

Once such a desire is inflamed, the individual becomes possessed with a yearning to seek it out. Individuals speak of an "insatiable quenching" within themselves, almost like they just cannot get enough of God. There is no concrete way to describe this reality. It is inside the person who knows it with a conviction no one can take away.

Desire leads to further desire. There is never enough. The more one has of God, the more one wants God. Desire thus expands the soul, enlarges the heart. Nikos Kazantzakis says it well:

"Never enough," Francis shouted. "It is not enough," Brother Leo. That is what God has shouted at me during these three days and nights, "Never enough." A poor man is made of clay and protests, "I cannot take any more," and God replies, "You can." And the man sighs, "I am going to burst." God replies, "Burst."[4]

I am reminded of Gerard Thomas Straub's personal story in his book *The Sun and Moon Over Assisi*. He writes of an experience in Rome:

> On the seat next to me was a prayer book.... My eyes were drawn to a psalm which began about halfway down the page. It was Psalm 63, and in bold print the text summarized the thrust of the psalm: "A Soul Thirsting for God."
>
> I read those few words and something happened, something mysterious and unexplainable: I began to cry, uncontrollably. I sat there and sobbed for at least five minutes. I was washed in the feeling that the entire trip was really a ruse to help me quench my soul's thirst for God. I read the psalm:
>
> > O God, you are my God, for you I long;
> > for you my soul is thirsting.
> > My body pines for you
> > like a dry, weary land without water.
> > So I gaze on you in the sanctuary
> > to see your strength and your glory...
>
> ...[A]s I read the above passage, my soul seemed enthusiastically to sing the words with great feeling and emotion, and without any concern for the fact that I didn't believe God existed.
>
> I closed the book. I looked at the tabernacle and prayed....
>
> After finishing the prayer, I was overtaken by a sense of peace, a peace which sprang from the sudden realization that God does exist, and, moreover, does love me. I felt as if I were floating in a sea of love. I closed my eyes and sat in tranquil silence for a few minutes. This was the moment of grace which changed my life.[5]

Bernard must have felt something similar. Without knowing it he invited Francis to his home because of a longing God awakened in his heart. The thirst for God is a yearning for intimacy that, once experienced, leaves one almost breathless and longing for more.

All Franciscans and all who visit Assisi are the continuation of that nightly encounter between Francis and Bernard. Like the first followers, we are "brothers and sisters of penance," brothers and sisters whose lives are formed by the gospel. Who Franciscans are today, and who they are called to be, had its origin in Bernard's home. Bonaventure writes:

> Therefore
> as the truth of the man of God's simple teaching and his life
> became known to many,
> some men began to be moved to penance
> and, abandoning all things,
> joined him in habit and life.
> The first among these was
> Bernard, a venerable man,
> who was made a sharer in the divine vocation
> and merited to be the firstborn son of the blessed Father,
> both in priority of time and in the gift of holiness. [6]

The house of Bernard still stands in Assisi at No. 10 on the Via Bernardo da Quintavalle, but this large family structure is not open to the public. Early on the graciousness of the family, particularly Signora Pennacchi when she was alive, had allowed us to visit there, climbing a short flight of stairs to a room designated to have been Bernard's bedroom that had been converted into a chapel. On numerous occasions our pilgrimage groups have been blessed with the opportunity to visit and celebrate Eucharist in that bedroom-chapel. This privilege is no longer ours. The family has put the house up for sale. But we can walk down the Via Bernardo da Quintavalle and pause before its front door. As we do perhaps we can hear our Good God awakening our hearts, offering us a treasure the likes of which no one else can give.

First Rule of Life
Church of San Nicolo

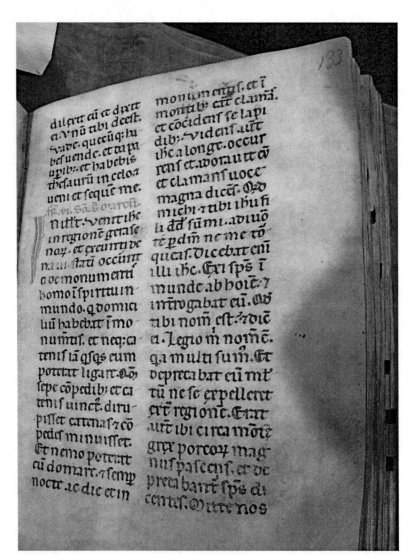

Because of Francis' experience on hearing the Gospel at the Porziuncola, February 24, 1208, he developed a confidence in the Word of God. This guided him as first he spent an evening with Bernard and then the following morning went to the Church of San Nicolo, together with Peter Catanio, to consult the Scriptures about what to do with their lives. *The Legend of the Three Companions* tells us what happened.

> Rising at daybreak, then, together with another man named Peter, who also wanted to become a brother, they went to the church of San Nicolo next to the piazza of the city of Assisi. They entered for prayer, but, because they were simple, they did not know how to find the passage in the Gospel about renunciation. They prayed devoutly that the Lord would show them his will on opening the book the first time....
>
> He desired it to be confirmed by a threefold affirmation. He opened the book a second and a third time.
>
> Each time he opened the book, blessed Francis thanked God for confirming his plan and the desire he had conceived earlier.[1]

These are the three texts that Francis opened up to:

> Jesus said to him, "If you wish to be perfect, go, sell your possessions, and give the money to the poor, and you will have treasure in heaven; then come, follow me." (Matthew 19:21)

> He said to them, "Take nothing for your journey, no staff, nor bag, nor bread, nor money—not even an extra tunic." (Luke 9:3)

Then Jesus told his disciples, "If any want to become my followers, let them deny themselves and take up their cross and follow me." (Matthew 16:24)

Placed side by side, these texts are stunning in their simplicity, starkness and power. A way of life was clearly defined and set before the three brothers. Try to image what was going on inside them. They intended to make a drastic change in their lives and embark upon a journey with far reaching consequences. After the third divine confirmation was clearly set forth, Francis said to Bernard and Peter, "Brothers, this is our life and rule and that of all who will want to join our company. Go, therefore, and fulfill what you have heard."[2] They trusted that God would guide them and show them the way.

This historical event took place very likely in 1208 or early 1209. We can confidently call this the First Rule of St. Francis of Assisi. Francis, Bernard and Peter became anchored in the direction their lives would take, and when the brothers numbered twelve they drew upon these Gospel texts to confidently craft a rule of life that they could present to the church for approval.

Francis' trust in God's Word would now sustain him for the rest of his life. He went on the road to proclaim the gospel. He proposed nothing to his brothers, the Poor Ladies and the laity of his time other than what he himself had discovered and put into practice.

The Missal of San Nicolo

The Missal of San Nicolo, which contained the Gospel texts that Francis, Bernard and Peter consulted to learn God's will, is still in existence. It is at the Walters Art Museum in Baltimore, Maryland. In early April, 2005, a companion and I had the opportunity for a private showing of the book. The curator, aware of our interest and purpose, gently and respectfully handled the missal, turning to the actual pages that Francis himself opened to. It was a moving and prayerful experience.

On one of the pages in the missal, written in red ink, the following declaration is made, which attests to the veracity of the missal:

> All (you) desiring to know, know this: That he (who goes by the) name "Gerard of Ugo"—and concerning whom this page is rightly kept is a partaker of every sacrifice and of all benefices which are celebrated by any one cleric or clerics in this, the church of blessed Nicolas. At the same time, he himself has worked tirelessly (to bring about) every good and useful (thing) for this aforementioned church. Wherefore, it seems proper and in accord with the Holy Scriptures that his remuneration is not good.[3]

This missal is dated by experts in paleography to the late twelfth century. Like many others of the time it was composed not only of texts for the celebration of the Eucharist, but also of Gospel passages. A good two-thirds of the book was made up of Gospel selections. The words "Gospels" and "missal" were frequently used interchangeably and thus it contained the passages that Francis took as the rule for his new order.

Don Aldo Brunacci, a distinguished Assisi historian, writes about it, "To me it seems there is no doubt. The missal surely belonged to the Church of San Nicolo *iuxta plateam civitatis Assisii.* It was in use during Saint Francis' youth. It is unthinkable that a little church could have had more than one missal for its use, because liturgical books, written by hand on parchment, were then very costly."[4]

The Church of San Nicolo was probably erected about the year 1000. Only the crypt remains as an entrance to an underground museum and pilgrims can get into the crypt for a historical visit. Whatever one's interest, the spirituality one might consider would simply be: *Trust in God's Word*. Francis, Bernard and Peter allowed the Word to take possession of their lives and then continued to act on it. Enjoy a cappuccino in the Piazza Comune, open the New Testament to one of the Gospels and welcome in the spirit.

13

Unfolding of Dreams and Birth
of an Order
St. John Lateran

In Franciscan history and tradition, St. John Lateran in Rome is sometimes called the Franciscan *Field of Dreams*. It is a place where dreams happened and where dreams were realized. Francis and the brothers had a dream of a new society and a new way to live the Gospel. This began with a dream or vision before a crucifix (San Damiano) with the words, "rebuild my church." Pope Innocent III also had a dream of the Lateran, the "mother church" of all Christianity, falling apart, and a beggar man holding it up. Innocent saw in his dream a future for the church that could be realized through these poor men from Assisi, that they could give flesh and meaning to a renewed church.

When Francis and Innocent met the two dreams came together and became real. Innocent and the church hierarchy wondered about Francis' vision and dream. Yet the zestful determination of Francis and the brothers was so expressive of the Spirit of God, they had no choice but to affirm the working of that Spirit, and the brothers came up with the practicalities that made their dreams come true.

In 1209 Francis and his first companions came to Rome to have their way of life, their dream, approved. Innocent III gave verbal approval to the brothers, tonsured them and commissioned them to preach penance. This fact is so vital because if Francis had not come to Pope Innocent III there would be no Franciscan family today. For this reason St. John Lateran is also called the baptistery of the Franciscan movement, the place where the Franciscan family was born.

Francis' life is sometimes aligned with other apostolic movements of his time that concentrated on Christ's missionary discourse to his apostles, encouraging his followers to go about the world with little or nothing. Duane Lapsanski, however, writes:

Francis also began his evangelical *metanoia* by observing these demands, as his biographers emphasize. But during the course of his life this evangelical seed blossomed into the observance of the *whole* Gospel.[1]

This could very well be some of the motivation that prompted Innocent III to give approval to this movement. Francis himself says in his Testament, "...the Most High himself made it clear to me that I must live *the life of the Gospel*." What we have is a deep-seated conviction on the part of Francis that he was called not simply to live a *part* of the gospel, say for example the missionary discourse, but rather the gospel of Jesus Christ, whole and entire, particularly the great commandment of love of God and neighbor. Duane Lapsanski further comments:

> For some unexplainable reason, the various lay movements of the twelfth and thirteenth centuries completely lost sight of the following of Christ and once again gave their full allegiance to the following of the apostles....
>
> With the coming of St. Francis and his followers, however, this "apostolic" element receded completely into the background and was replaced by a renewed emphasis on the following of *Christ*. Though many elements in the life of the Friars Minor closely resembled that of the earlier movements, their motivation and inspiration for living this kind of life were significantly different. Whereas the life of the *apostles* and the *example of the early Church* were the primary goals of most religious groups of these centuries, it was clearly the following of *Christ himself* which inspired the Friars Minor....
>
> By following directly in the footsteps of Christ they were not interested in restoring the *early* Church but rather in reforming their *contemporary* Church.[2]

Because the Crucified Christ became so central a reality to Francis' life, his sights were set only on Christ, no one else. Because of his rootedness in Christ, Francis could embrace the church as an institution, despite her shortcomings. To embrace the church, for Francis, was to embrace Christ.

It is true that there was a troubled relationship between the church and other apostolic movements of the time, but Francis planted himself firmly on the side of the church. It is hard to imagine any two different men than Francis on the one hand and Innocent III, and even Bishop Guido of Assisi, on the other. But Francis saw in them the successors of the apostles who received their authority from God. This made all the difference to him.

We can ask the question: Why did the pope listen to Francis and confirm his way of life? Prior to Francis ever meeting Innocent, we know that something had been happening to Francis and this is what made the pope listen. Two factors stand out.

The first is Francis' experience of God, his months and years in the caves around Assisi. One man went in, another came out, affecting an interior change that forced the pope to notice. World leaders today listened to other such "God-visited" persons, like Mother Teresa, John Paul II and Gandhi. They had undergone such interior change that others were compelled to listen. Francis had an interior silence that rose out of making hard decisions for God. The interior quietness made it easy for the pope, to see, to listen. Innocent knew that here was a God-spirited man and was bound to confirm Francis' proposal and send him forth for the church.

The second is Francis' utter honesty or confidence. Francis saw himself as dependent, little, nothing on his own, but grew in the awareness that he is good, strong and self-assured only because of his God. He began to be honest about his feelings and image of self. Murray Bodo once made the comment, "All great persons know they are great; otherwise they lie and are dishonest to self and others."

It was humility, learned in the caves, and the experience of littleness and dependence, that kept a proper perspective and balance. It was Francis' experience of God that didn't allow greatness to turn into pride, power, arrogance or cruelty.

One time Innocent asked Francis to pray that God might reveal his will regarding Francis' request. God spoke to Francis figuratively through the image of a poor woman living in the desert with her sons. He returned to the supreme pontiff and narrated the story God revealed. "My Lord," he said, "I am that little poor woman whom the loving Lord, in His mercy, has adorned, and through whom He has been pleased to give birth to legitimate sons. The King of kings has told me that He will nourish all the sons born to me, because, if He feeds strangers, He must provide for His own."[3]

This depicts Francis' assurance of self, growing out of his experience of God. Francis says: God has called me; God has revealed to me; God is leading me. I am that woman; I am giving birth. I know this with certainty. This changes the picture of Francis as a simpleton in the sense of someone ignorant and unlearned. It changes the picture of how Francis understood littleness and nothingness. It led to confidence because of the way God touched him. This sealed Francis' identity within and gave force to his honesty, all of which compelled the pope to listen and confirm what God was doing.

So to answer the question, "Why did Innocent listen to Francis?" we are forced to return to the person of Francis. It was impossible not to be drawn to him by his genuineness and humility. He had no hidden agenda. All he desired was to imitate Christ and this completely disarmed any adversaries. To say no to Francis would have seemed like saying no directly to Christ. Francis broke down any defense mechanisms of those he met; his simplicity was irresistible.

Perhaps we might want to consider that in order to enter into an effective relationship between obedience and authority, we must be able to offer something for confirmation, something interior that would compel the other to listen. This could mean a life that is so changed, so filled with inner light, by the experience of God that it begins to exude an inner dynamism that attracts the other to listen. It could mean a life that displays such utter honesty of self before others that again others are attracted to listen by the sheer power of littleness and humility.

Francis did not allow the church to be a hard rock, unbending or lifeless. Rather, he found himself reborn in and through the church as a mother giving birth. How can we bring life to the church in our time? How to rebuild and yet stay within the institution? How to transform from within? How to make a hard rock soft, pliable and life-giving? How can we be pregnant with Jesus?

St. John Lateran is more closely connected with the life of Francis and the whole Franciscan movement than any other place in Rome. In visiting this basilica, think of Francis' genuineness, humility and simplicity as well as one's own relationship to the church. Consider the inner spirit that Francis brought to Innocent that made him irresistible. It is that spirit that gives birth to dreams and gives us the courage to step into the future with confidence and hope.

14

Prayer and Mountain Spirituality
Poggio Bustone

Poggio Bustone is the most northern and highest sanctuary in the Rieti Valley. It is perhaps the most impressive of all the Franciscan places in this region, set as it is in a high, rugged and remote area. The surrounding mountains cast a mystical spell over anyone who ascends its heights, whether it be by bus, car or on foot. Its setting for prayer is unmistakable. Francis, it is said, found a small deserted hermitage on his first visit, probably in 1209 after his meeting with Innocent III. Delighted by the loneliness of the spot, he took possession of it for himself and his brothers.

Poggio Bustone lends itself to a consideration of what one might call "mountain spirituality." Moses first met God on a mountain in his experience of the burning bush. He descended with a commission from God to liberate the people from slavery in Egypt. After this Passover from Egypt was completed, Moses went up and came down from Mount Sinai with the law for the regulation of the people's religious, civil and social life.

Elijah was overwhelmed by God on Mount Horeb. We know the story well.

[The Lord came to Elijah and said:] "Go out and stand on the mountain before the Lord, for the Lord is about to pass by." Now there was a great wind, so strong that it was splitting mountains and breaking rocks in pieces before the Lord, but the Lord was not in the wind; and after the wind an earthquake, but the Lord was not in the earthquake; and after the earthquake a fire, but the Lord was not in the fire; and after the fire a sound of sheer silence. When Elijah heard it, he wrapped his face in his mantle and went out and stood at the entrance of the cave. Then there came a voice to him that said, "What are you doing here, Elijah?" (1 Kings 19:11–13)

The stories of Moses and Elijah give us examples of the extraordinary spirit and dynamism associated with mountains, as if somehow on a mountain one could encounter the presence of God more readily. There is a mysticism that seems to beckon every courageous soul.

Mountains are particularly important in Matthew's Gospel. Jesus preaches a sermon on one (chapters 5—7) and is transfigured on one (chapter 17). Jesus goes to a mountain alone to pray (chapter 14), and prayer on a mountain is the onset of his suffering (chapter 21). Jesus' last words to his followers are delivered from a mountain as he commissions his disciples for their work in continuation of his own (chapter 28). In their mission the followers of Jesus are the embodiment of Jesus' mountain revelation. Matthew's picture of Jesus is that of a new Moses, bringing freedom and new life.

In a similar fashion mountains are important in Francis' life. Francis experienced God on a mountain at Poggio Bustone. Francis was inspired to finalize his Rule from a mountain at Fonte Colombo, another sanctuary in the Rieti Valley. Francis was also inspired to reenact Bethlehem on a mountain at Greccio. Francis met Christ crucified on a mountain at La Verna. Francis experienced God in prayer on numerous other mountains: the Carceri, Speco di Narni, Bellegra, Celle di Cortona, to name a few.

On Poggio Bustone, for example, Francis was drawn out of himself and came to a deep, convincing awareness and certainty of the magnitude of God's compassion. Celano writes:

> One day he was marveling at the Lord's mercy in the kindness shown to him. He wished that the Lord would show him the course of life for him and his brothers, and he went to a place of prayer (Poggio Bustone), as he so often did....

He began to lose himself;

his feelings were pressed together;

and that darkness disappeared

which fear of sin had gathered in his heart.

Certainty of the forgiveness of all his sins poured in,

and the assurance of being revived in grace was given to

him.

Then he was caught up above himself and totally engulfed in

light,

and, with his inmost soul opened wide,

he clearly saw the future.

As that sweetness and light withdrew,

renewed in spirit,

he now seemed to be *changed into another man.*[1]

Notice the expressions: "he began to lose himself"..."he was totally engulfed in light"..."his inmost soul opened wide"..."he now seemed to be changed into another man." It seems that he cannot help but be drawn into the embrace of an omnipotent, yet tender, God.

Poggio Bustone affords one the opportunity to "climb a mountain" and enter into mountain spirituality. Climbing a mountain makes us aware of our burdens and perhaps all the baggage we carry throughout life. We begin to sort out what is necessary and what we can let go of. The reduced baggage allows God to draw us into mystery and contemplation, as God did for Moses, Elijah, Jesus and Francis.

The spirituality of Poggio Bustone, or "mountain spirituality," calls forth deep contemplative prayer. Heart-centered prayer, or contemplation, is not so much our praying or speaking to God as it is becoming aware that it is God who is pursuing us and praying in us, drawing us upward. All of Scripture reveals this wonderful mystery of our God. It is God who comes in search of us; it is God who desires us, desires to be one with us; it is God who loves us with passionate longing. It is God who comes to us with overwhelming compassion.

Francis prayed in many ways, but the stories of his life and his descriptions of God are such that again and again it was the experience of a man who had become overpowered, possessed by God. It was the experience of one who allowed God to pray in him, change him, empower him, overwhelm him, who knew nothing could ever separate him from the love of God given to us through his Son. Over and over again Francis called God "Most High." He seemed to be stretching physically for his Lord. Anyone who enjoys the opportunity for climbing a mountain might imagine oneself doing the same.

When most pilgrims come to Poggio Bustone, they get as far as Convento San Giacomo, which was founded in 1217. The center of the sanctuary, however, is reached by a challenging half-hour climb up the mountain. Here one comes upon the remains of a small chapel where Francis and the early brothers spent time. Anyone who has the stamina to make the climb should do so. It offers a more complete spiritual experience of a mountain. We can touch into the feelings of awe, grandeur and power. We can allow the mountain to overtake us, draw us up and overwhelm us so that we are led to silence. Our spirit can then begin to absorb the presence of God and the power of praying within. Nothing else will matter.

[15]

The Gift of Fraternity
Rivo Torto

Rivo Torto is a place that holds many memories of the earliest years of the Franciscan story. It is about two miles from the Porziuncola, St. Mary of the Angels and two miles from Assisi. It is the site of the huts or sheds that housed the first friars. The abandoned shed that the brothers discovered was called a *tugurio*, considered by the peasants to be the poorest possible farmhouse. The shed was near a crooked stream, a *rivo torto*, which was simply a drainage ditch collecting water from the surrounding mountains. Nevertheless, it was home for the brothers, and the stories that have come down to us remind us that these first days together were like the honeymoon period of the Franciscan Order. The love and care that the brothers knew left an indelible imprint on their memory.

The following stories are worth retelling.

In their zeal to be perfect and purify themselves, in imitation of blessed Francis, the new community of friars enthusiastically fasted with great severity. Once, however, a young friar awoke screaming in the middle of the night saying that he was dying of hunger. Our father Francis immediately woke all the other friars and admonished: "Do not imitate me. You must find Christ in your own way. God created us as a brotherhood and he created us in his individual likeness. Each friar must allow his body its needs so that it has the strength to serve the spirit. While we are bound to avoid overindulgence, which injures both body and soul, we must also avoid excessive abstinence" The tender father then took some grapes which they had received the previous day, and in his knightly courtesy, he encouraged all the friars to eat together so as not to embarrass the one who awoke with the complaint. Throughout the night they ate and laughed and told stories, as they were often given to do,

transforming that hovel of Rivotorto into a veritable ban-
quet hall.[1]

Another comes to us from *The Legend of the Three Companions.*

> The blessed father with his sons were staying in a place near
> Assisi called Rivo Torto where there was a hut abandoned by
> all. The place was so cramped that they could barely sit or
> rest. Very often for lack of bread, their only food was the
> turnips that they begged in their need, here and there.
>
> The man of God would write the names of the brothers
> on the beams of that hut, so that anyone wishing to rest or
> pray would know his place, and so that any unusual noise
> would not disturb the mind's silence in such small and
> close quarters.[2]

The glue that held the brothers together was respect and genuine
love. Whenever Christ spoke about love, he seemed to talk about
responding to others in such a way that we would allow others into
our lives and give them a right to make demands on us, because we
chose to love. We could allow them to use us, because we chose to
love. Likewise, in allowing God to be intimate with us, we gave God
a right to make demands and hold us accountable. When Jesus
asked Peter, "Do you love me?" and Peter responded with a
resounding "Yes!" the Lord in effect said to him, "I tell you, when
you were younger, you used to fasten your own belt and to go wherever you wished. But when you grow old, you will stretch out your
hands, and someone else will fasten a belt around you and take you
where you do not wish to go" (John 21:18). Peter's greatness would
unfold in a lifetime of response to such a challenge. Or we know
well the scene of the last judgment in Matthew 25. The poor, the
hungry, the thirsty, the homeless had a right to expect their needs

to be met, because they had a right to expect to find loving people, empowered with the Spirit of God.

How do we receive those persons in our life who make demands on us? We who are the ministers of the brothers or sisters, we who are teachers in classrooms, or pastoral ministers, or mothers and fathers? How do we welcome those members of the human race who sometimes, like Peter experienced, lead us where we would prefer not to go, and ask us to do what we don't want to do? How do we receive those who use us?

Murray Bodo said to me one day, "You never see a tired selfish person." Such are always taking care of themselves, making sure their needs are met.

If we choose to love, if we decide to accept the demands of being a loving person, we immediately take on the responsibility of being *for* others, in service and in times of opposition, in trials and persecution, also in peace and joy. We accept this dynamic not in the way we would like, but as determined by the needs of others around us. Frequently, this means putting more heart into what we are about in all the ordinary tasks of daily life; it means reaching deeper into the source of our energy when it seems like it is too hard to allow the ministry or a child or another to keep making demands. It takes a self-possessed, mature person to respond thus. But these same people know freedom; they are free from self and free for others, free to live the challenge of the gospel and open to the most that life can call forth. Such know joy!

Saint Francis de Sales once said, "The measure of love is to love without measure."[3] This is a clever way to describe or define this essential fact of Christian life. Each of us knows how easy it is to measure out the giving of ourselves to another, and to think these are expressions of love. I'm sure they are. But often we keep track.

We count how many times we telephoned another, how many times we took out the garbage, how many times we did the dishes or cleaned up after others, how many times we drove the kids to school or events, how many times we led prayer in the friary or volunteered to cook a meal. We count; we measure.

We do the same with God: "God, I've said so many prayers, made so many sacrifices. Don't you think, God, it's your turn to answer and do something?"

Fraternity and the genuine love that lies at its foundation, as for any environment that requires love as its binding force, is first of all a quality of the heart and grows out of the conviction that we do not exist for ourselves but for the kingdom of God. Genuine love results from our capacity to make the interests of others more important than our own.

Francis and the brothers knew a special kind of love at Rivo Torto. What bound the brothers together was the conviction that they willingly and firmly professed the same gospel values and vision of life. Each was committed to the gospel of love, even trying to outdo each other in showing it. Perhaps a visit to this sacred place can inspire us to grow in the gift, the challenges and the demands and joys of love.

16

A Heart for the Brotherhood
Porziuncola

The brothers remained at Rivo Torto only until a poor farmer moved in one day with his donkey. Then they moved on to St. Mary of the Angels, the Little Portion. Even though Rivo Torto was the first setting for the new fraternity in the Assisi region, it was at the Porziuncola, St. Mary of the Angels, that the Franciscan story unfolded. Together with San Damiano there are no more important places in the original Franciscan story than these two. That is why it is so important to visit and return to these sanctuaries again and again. This is Francis' heart; this is Francis' center and the center of the entire Franciscan story.

Why?

- Here Francis began his religious life, understanding his vocation and life direction through the hearing of the Gospel.
- Here his life and vocation developed.
- Here it ended when he died on October 3, 1226.
- Here the first brotherhood developed and flourished around a small chapel in the woods with rush huts nearby.
- Here chapters (regular meetings held perhaps twice a year) took place and critical decisions were made. To this day general chapters gather friars here from all over the world.
- From here the brothers were sent out on mission to preach (Italy, Europe, the world) with a message of peace and reconciliation.
- Here they returned to share their faith, their experiences and to be nourished.
- Here a definite lifestyle grew and developed, and a formation into Franciscan life took place.
- Here Francis received the promise of the pardon (Il Perdono) from Jesus Christ through Mary. We know this as the Porziuncola Indulgence. When asked why he wanted this, he answered, "I want to send everyone to Paradise."

• Here on Palm Sunday night, 1212, Clare was received into the community and her hair shorn.

• Here Francis and Clare shared a meal and in their conversation it seemed a fire was consuming the entire area.

• Here Francis repaired a little church with his own hands, these being the very stones he laid, worn smooth now by millions of passing pilgrims throughout the centuries.

• Here Francis discovered Jesus; here he discovered poverty, humility; here he discovered Mary, and his heart, and the heart of his brotherhood, would be forever rooted in the ways of the gospel.

For these reasons the Porziuncola is the heart and center of Francis, the core of the Franciscan movement; it is the womb from which it grew. This is truly holy ground.

Today the original Porziuncola Chapel rests in the center of a much larger structure, the Basilica of St. Mary of the Angels, built hundreds of years after the death of Saint Francis. The chapel is well preserved so that visitors can experience this place much like Francis did in the early thirteenth century. The setting of the original chapel in the large basilica is a center that reflects one's soul, wherein one finds beauty and truth, peace and forgiveness. It is as if the very core of one's being is exposed for all to see and experience, a space within that has no boundaries or restrictions so that the spirit may soar. It is the place we call "heart."

Bonaventure writes:

This place
the holy man loved more than other places in the world;
for here he began humbly,
here he progressed virtuously,
here he ended happily.

> This place
> he entrusted to his brothers at his death....
> This is the place
> where the Order of Lesser Brothers
> was begun by Saint Francis
> under the prompting of divine revelation.[1]

The very setting of this chapel cannot but help us image a center. We know we can make any number of idols our center: our work, our value system or a relationship. When we are physically within the chapel itself, it is like entering the heart of the gospel that calls us again to clarify our center, to realize that Jesus alone is the true center of life and that he is the one who gives meaning to the way we relate to all the other facets: work, values, people.

Saint Paul, for example, was unmistakably clear in his vision:

> I regard everything as loss because of the surpassing value of knowing Christ Jesus my Lord. For his sake I have suffered the loss of all things, and I regard them as rubbish, in order that I may gain Christ and be found in him....
>
> I want to know Christ and the power of his resurrection....
>
> Not that I have already obtained this or have already reached the goal; but I press on to make it my own, because Christ Jesus has made me his own.
>
> ...[T]his one thing I do: forgetting what lies behind and straining forward to what lies ahead. (Philippians 3:8–9, 10, 12, 13)

One cannot help but be mesmerized by the energy Paul is exerting for Christ. Jesus is his center and pulling force. Jesus is the reason for all this energy. Our presence at the Porziuncola is telling us the same: Jesus is to be the center and motivating force of our lives. The whole purpose of life hinges on that, the whole purpose. We can do all things and be involved in many ministries, but if we fail to know Jesus as a center, as our goal, we lose the race.

When Francis understood his vocation at the Porziuncola as he listened to the Gospel in February, 1208, he cried out, "This is what I wish; this is what I seek; this is what I long to do with all my heart."[2] Go to St. Mary of the Angels, the Porziuncola. Upon entering the huge basilica one is drawn to the little chapel. One's heart senses the invitation to come in and dwell awhile. Feel the stones, pick up the spiritual energy present here and once more understand the importance of having a heart, a center.

17

True Poverty Versus False Poverty
San Francesco a Ripa

When Francis visited Rome on a number of occasions, he generally
lodged where the poor were gathered. Since at the time many poor
and sick were in the Trastevere region of Rome, he frequently,
according to tradition, would find his way there to live and minister among them. We are told that in 1219 the Benedictines gave a
place to Saint Francis and his companions. This became the friars'
first residence in Rome. Originally named the Hospital of St. Blase,
the property passed into the hands of the fraternity in 1229 by order
of the pope and eventually was renamed San Francesco a Ripa. It is
now a small parish church served by the friars, and the structure
preserves a small cell above the sacristy to commemorate the visits
that Saint Francis made to this place.

Regarding the spirituality connected with San Francesco a
Ripa, the obvious focus would be on the economically poor and the
outcasts of society. To respond to their needs and to live as they do,
would give tangible shape to one of Francis' greatest desires, the
commitment to poverty. There is another dimension, however, that
can be easily missed. It too rests at the heart of Francis' thinking.
We can call it "poverty of being," or "ontological poverty," namely
that which defines essentially who I am. This is the kind of poverty
Francis wanted, more than anything, to instill into his brothers.
Without the embrace and integration of this truth, a life of material
poverty had little or no foundation.

Ilia Delio writes:

Poverty is rooted in one's existence as creature and the
knowledge that one is not equal to God. Poverty means radical dependency, recognizing one's utter dependency on
God. When I ask the question, "who am I?" I begin a life of
poverty because the answer is one of radical dependency. I
am not the source of my own life; rather, I come from God

and belong to God. To be created by God is to enjoy a graced nature. However, because I am created out of nothing, I have a tendency towards nothingness. Simply by being human, therefore, I am poor because I am dependent on God for the very existence of my being.[1]

Being a human creature is who I am and therefore defines me. To focus only, or primarily, on material poverty can result in a false poverty. If I do that I can sidetrack the need to grow in purity of heart, which is the key to poverty of being. One must be very cautious here. The Incarnational dimension of poverty (the physical or material expression) is vital. One can relegate it to a nonexistent status by claiming, "I'm focusing on my poverty of being," and miss the poor and outcasts in our midst. On the other hand, it is easy to dedicate one's life to the poor and feel good about it. Without the foundation, however, of knowing and accepting the poverty we all have as human creatures, something critical is lacking, and ministry to the poor, as also a simplicity in lifestyle, can quickly become self-serving and eventually lose stamina.

This is why Francis repeatedly spoke to his brothers about purity of heart. Francis saw poverty as a basic attitude of the entire person. It included material poverty in the form of emptying one's heart of all attachment to earthly goods. Francis also wanted his followers to empty their hearts of all immaterial goods as well, that is, of all values of which a person can be inwardly proud. Francis encouraged the brothers to let go of other inner possessions such as anxieties of the heart, anger, hatred, envy, ambition or any attitude that turned one's attention to the self. And finally, Francis wanted his brothers to empty their hearts of all spiritual security as well. He wanted his brothers to stand naked before God with outstretched arms, in complete nakedness of spirit.

Francis called this "purity of heart" and it is the one reality above all others that he consistently called the brothers to embody. This teaching shows up in one after another of his *Admonitions*, highlighted in the following selections.

Admonition XIV: Poverty of Spirit
Blessed are the poor in spirit, for theirs is the kingdom of heaven.
There are many who, while insisting on prayers and obligations, inflict many abstinences and punishments upon their bodies. But they are immediately offended and disturbed about a single word which seems to be harmful to their bodies or about something which might be taken away from them. These people are not poor in spirit, for someone who is truly poor in spirit hates himself and loves those who strike him on the cheek.[2]

Admonition XIII: Patience
Blessed are the peacemakers, for they will be called children of God.
A servant of God cannot know how much patience and humility he has within himself as long as he is content. When the time comes, however, when those who should make him content do the opposite, he has as much patience and humility as he has at that time and no more.[3]

Admonition XXII: Correction
Blessed is the servant who endures discipline, accusation, and reprimand from another as patiently as he would from himself.

Blessed is the servant who, after being reprimanded, agrees courteously, submits respectfully, admits humbly, and makes amends willingly.

> Blessed is the servant who is not quick to excuse him-
> self, and endures with humility, shame, and reprimand for
> a sin, when he did not commit the fault.[4]

Each of these is a description of "poverty of spirit" and offers an insight into the mystery of becoming "pure of heart." The frequency with which Francis presents this advice to the brothers speaks to the centrality of his comprehension of the human person. It expresses an interior acceptance and integration into life of being a creature, God's creature, thus describing "poverty of being," or "ontological poverty."

This is the basis of true poverty that frees the individual to give all and seek only the kingdom of God. One could pursue a false poverty if this foundation was bypassed by concentrating primarily on expressions of material poverty.

How does one grow in purity of heart and therefore ontological poverty? One of the essential criteria is a rhythm of daily prayer. Prayer affords one the opportunity to acknowledge, day after day, that God alone is God and that I am God's creature, dependent on God for everything. In prayer one must beg God each day to move one's heart to welcome this treasure. It is impossible to embrace it on one's own power. Another important—and for Franciscans, essential—factor is "life in fraternity" or simply community life or family life, a privileged place for an encounter with God. Here one must face and deal with the demands of love, the demands of service, the give and take of daily living. One's response to this is the actual realm for growing in purity of heart and a transformation of spirit. Within this context of life together the practicalities of material poverty can be espoused: for example, the sharing of resources, support for one another's journey in faith, ministry and responsibilities. Herein one can experience trust in a loving and tender God and trust in one's brothers or sisters. It becomes possible then to "appropriate nothing to oneself."

One might conclude that the above is a nice dream and rarely attainable. Yet when we look at Francis, this is what poverty meant to him. This is the poverty he wanted above all. Material poverty was not his primary goal. Rather he wanted his followers to come to grips with poverty of being. It was this concern Francis focused on again and again. "Material poverty is only sacramental of the deeper poverty of being human."[5] Unfortunately, the brothers quickly lost sight of this aspect of poverty since many of their struggles focused on the issues of material poverty. Material poverty and "appropriating nothing to oneself" are critical dimensions of life, but to stop there and see the whole picture of poverty largely from that perspective is to embrace a false poverty.

The pilgrim hallowed with the opportunity to visit San Francesco a Ripa in Rome can either spend some time in the little church or ask the sacristan to visit the room above that holds the memory of Francis' presence. In quiet prayer ask our God to clarify one's vision about the meaning of poverty and to be blessed with the grace to embrace poverty of being, namely the poverty that comes from being a creature of God. Out of this one's response to the economically poor and the outcasts of society can be entered into with a freedom and excitement only few know.

18

Preaching the Word of God
Cathedral of San Rufino

From the standpoint of the Franciscan story, the Cathedral of San Rufino in the upper part of Assisi holds the memory of several significant events. It preserves the baptistery in which both Francis and Clare received the waters of baptism and the gift of faith in Jesus Christ. Documents in the San Rufino archives indicate that Clare's family home was just to the left of this building. It was from that home that Clare made her way at midnight on Palm Sunday, 1212, to join Francis and the brothers at the Porziuncola in the valley below. On occasion Francis also preached in this cathedral and one might well imagine that one of his hearers was the young woman, Clare. His words touched her heart to the point that she eventually embodied the vision and ideals of Francis in a way unmatched by any other.

A little known fact, however, is that when Francis was invited to preach on a Sunday in the Cathedral he would spend the previous Saturday night in prayer, preparing his heart and spirit to speak the words that God inspired within. There is a little chapel below the sacristy in the cathedral. It is not open to visitors, but it preserves the memory of the place where Francis prepared what God inspired him to speak. Bonaventure writes:

> While the brothers were still staying in the place already mentioned, one Saturday the holy man entered the city of Assisi to preach in the cathedral on Sunday morning, as was his custom. In a hut situated in the garden of the canons, away from his sons in body, the man devoted to God spent the night in his customary way, in the prayer of God.[1]

What must be understood about Francis is the centrality of the Word of God in his life. The Word became flesh, Incarnate. The mystery of the Incarnation engraved itself upon Francis' heart like a seal pressed into hot wax. This is the defining hallmark of the Franciscan gift to Christian spirituality, namely, that God became one of us. This truth inspired Francis' prayer, his words, his life, his mission and all his activity. Reading and absorbing Scripture for Francis was meeting Jesus on the road. Francis was so intent on the Gospel because it was an encounter with the living Incarnate Christ. One must take this into account to understand why Francis prepared the way he did for the task of preaching. He tasted the Word; he breathed the Word; he became the embodiment of the Word so that when people saw and heard him preach, they were not simply hearing words about peace or reconciliation, mercy or love or forgiveness, but they were in the presence of a living Gospel; they were in the presence of one who made the Word incarnate in his own life.

Faith and prayer are indispensable for making the Word one's source of life. Through faith and prayer the preacher lets God come into the world. When people sense that the preacher is one who believes, who lives with God, faith and hope become a reality for them as well. Doors open up and the listeners begin to suspect it really is possible to believe. Faith comes alive as people sense a hunger being filled in their own hearts. People believed in Francis because what he preached was lived and authenticated in his life.

Thomas of Celano has a wonderful passage about Francis' understanding of Sacred Scripture and the power of his words. He writes:

> Although this blessed man
> was not educated in scholarly disciplines,
> still he learned from God *wisdom from above*
> and, enlightened by the splendors of eternal light,
> he understood Scripture deeply.

His genius, pure and unstained,

penetrated *hidden mysteries*.

Where the knowledge of teachers is outside,

the passion of the lover entered.

He sometimes read the Sacred Books,

and whatever he once put into his mind,

he *wrote* indelibly *in his heart*.

His memory took the place of books,

because, if he heard something once,

it was not wasted,

as his heart would mull it over with constant devotion.

He said this was the fruitful way to read and learn,

rather than to wander through a thousand treatises.

. . .

Unskilled in words,

he spoke splendidly with understanding and power.[2]

This pattern of life served as a backdrop for the power and spirit in Francis' preaching. As we learn from Francis, the first task of one who proclaims and explains the Word of God is that the person be grounded in a God-experience that is nurtured in prayer. None of this comes automatically; it must be lived. Francis' preaching was effective because he lived the Word. He pondered the Word; he nurtured the Word; he became the embodiment of the Word. And thus when he proclaimed the Word, people saw the Word come to life.

19

Clare: Risking All, the First Step
Porta Moiano

Children sometimes play a game of dare. They dare, or double dare, each other to do things all the time as part of their play. It could be as simple as wading through a puddle after a heavy rainfall, or climbing a billboard, or crossing a busy street. Today it could be members of a street gang daring someone to shoot. These games strengthen the ego identity of the darer and challenge the courage of the one dared. Usually the dare is innocent enough although sometimes it could involve dire consequences as often seen in college hazing or street gang activities.

On Palm Sunday night in 1212 Clare responded to a dare that changed her life forever. She dared to listen to the inspiration of God; she dared to accept the gospel as her only treasure; she dared to embrace a vision of life that Francis held out to her. *The Legend of Saint Clare* describes the event briefly.

> On that night, preparing to obey the command of the saint, she embarked upon her long desired flight with a virtuous companion. Since she was not content to leave by way of the usual door, marveling at her strength, she broke open with her own hands that other door that is customarily blocked by wood and stone.[1]

To help us understand the profundity of this step, consider for a moment another scene in Matthew's account (14:22–33) of Jesus walking on water and inviting Peter to come to him. We know the story: Jesus just fed five thousand; he dismissed the crowds, sent the disciples on their way across the sea, went off to pray and then came walking on the water toward them as they battled a storm. This occasioned an encounter with Peter, who said, "Lord, if it is you, command me to come to you on the water." Peter dared Jesus and in turn Jesus dared Peter to see and believe. He simply said,

"Come." And that's exactly what Peter did. He stepped out of the boat and began to walk across those rolling waters with his eyes fixed on Jesus. Imagine that first step! Imagine the risk and the courage, fleeting as it may have been.

I think of Clare's first step out of her home as she left to join Francis. Not knowing what was to happen, she made the decision to risk all and trust in a future based on God's promises. God in effect said to Clare, "Come, walk on water, trust my word." And that's what Clare did. Imagine her first step!

The scene in the Gospel also called forth faith from Peter. At first glance Peter failed miserably. Why? He was already halfway to Jesus when he took his eyes off Jesus and looked instead at the crashing waves and heard the roaring wind, and then said to himself, "This is crazy. I can't walk on water." He sank like a rock. But he had indeed walked on water. He had been able to do the impossible, because his eyes were fixed on Jesus, and because his heart, his whole heart, was fixed on Jesus too. Walking on water only became impossible for Peter when he looked away from the Lord.

Clare must have had moments of doubt about her decision in the years that followed. We know, however, how steadfastly she maintained her gaze upon Jesus, always finding in that gaze clarity of purpose and conviction in her chosen path. The good news about Peter is that doubt did not lead to drowning but deeper faith. Likewise for Clare.

Like the invitation of Peter and Clare, Jesus is inviting us to walk on water and do the impossible: to build wonderful lives and wonderful friendships, not off in some safe, otherworldly haven, but here and now in the midst of all the troubles and tragedies that life can serve us. The reason so many of us sink and are drowned in our troubles, or sink beneath the waves and turmoil of our difficulties is that we take our eyes off Jesus and begin to rely only on ourselves.

How do we find the power to walk on water and do the impossible? Exactly as Peter and Clare did, by keeping our eyes and hearts fixed on Jesus. He will show us where to walk and will give us the energy and courage to walk there. We will not falter or sink into the sea as long as our eyes and hearts are set on him. And he promises more than mere survival as the waters rage and the winds howl around us. He promises us joy and peace, even while life is battering us.

On many of the Franciscan Pilgrimage Programs, the group is led in a touching and powerful ritual. We call it "Clare's Ritual of Departure." Shortly after dusk has fallen, we gather in the Piazza of San Rufino near what would have been Clare's paternal home. From there until the Porta Moiano, one of the eight gates of the city, we wend our way through Assisi in the dark, making six or seven stops to reflect on what might have been going on in Clare's heart and thoughts. She made the momentous decision to leave her home and join Francis' movement as the first Franciscan woman. Imagine the blackness of night; imagine the firmness of her decision; imagine the trepidation and fear that also must have filled her spirit; imagine her first step. But Clare, with a trusted companion, silently made her way to the ancient Porta Moiano, a departure from the city of her birth. Some of the brothers were waiting just outside the gate with torches to take her to Francis at the Porziuncola below.

Testimony from Clare's Process of Canonization indicates that her home bordered the Piazza of San Rufino. Tradition also tells us that Saint Clare's grandfather, Offreduccio, donated part of the land in front of his manor house for the enlargement of the new cathedral of San Rufino. Historians use this to demonstrate that

Clare's paternal home was very near the cathedral, just to the left of it. Very likely the cathedral was the parish church for the family.

When in Assisi, walk up the hill from the Piazza Comune to the Piazza of San Rufino. Imagine Clare risking all by taking that first step to join Francis. Read Matthew 14:22–33 and compare Peter's first step onto the water with Clare's first step out of her paternal home. Take a slow walk through the city, preferably at night, and head for the Porta Moiano. It is a gate not used by many. On passing through the gate, there is total darkness. Light a candle and spend some minutes recalling Clare's departure from home.

Hear God's invitation to risk all for the sake of the kingdom. What might be the first step to take?

20

A New Look at Contemplation
San Damiano[1]

The two places most closely aligned with Saint Francis are San Damiano and St. Mary of the Angels. Yet the person most associated with San Damiano is Clare. When Francis brought Clare to San Damiano in 1212, she would remain there for the next forty-one years. Margaret Carney calls Clare "The First Franciscan Woman," and rightly so. She modeled Francis' vision more closely than any other. It is Clare's presence at San Damiano that is the key to coming to know Francis even more so than through the first brothers. After Francis died, Clare carried on his vision. She lived a life of poverty like no other, a life of prayer, penance, service, love and healing, a life of evangelical perfection. The brothers would come to her for spiritual guidance as they struggled to make Francis' vision a reality. She gave a whole new image to the women of her time and was properly called "the new woman of the Spoleto Valley."

Perhaps Clare's greatest gift to the Franciscan story and to the church is a new, refreshing way to look at contemplation. Contemplation for Francis and Clare was a matter of vision, a matter of where one focused his or her gaze. The goal of the monk of that time was to gaze upward toward heaven and this upward direction would lead to union with God. The goal for the Franciscan, on the other hand, was a penetrating gaze into the ordinary of life. The starting point is the Incarnation, God descending to us rather than our ascending to God. Our gaze is upon this Incarnate God as reflected, particularly, in the Crucified Lord. The goal of contemplation for a monk focused on a vision of God that resulted in the ecstatic union. The goal of contemplation for the Franciscan focused on transformation by which one became like the face of God reflected in the Incarnation. The following diagram is perhaps helpful. Think of it as an ascending or descending ladder.

Monastic Focus	Franciscan Focus
4. Contemplation	1. Gaze
3. Prayer	2. Consider
2. Meditation	3. Contemplate
1. Reading	4. Imitate

For the monk the journey began at the bottom of the ladder, moving upward from sacred reading to meditation to prayer and finally contemplative union. The Franciscan, on the other hand, saw God descending to become one like us, and one discovered the face of God in that descent that revealed itself in poverty, humility and compassionate charity. Contemplative union for the monk was a goal to be achieved only in heaven, or by being drawn out of oneself apart from any contact with the world. Contemplative union in the Franciscan tradition happened in the process of transformation into the image of the Incarnate Lord in the here and now.

Clare, perhaps more than Francis, offered us a way of understanding this approach when she wrote to Agnes of Prague:

> Your Spouse, though more beautiful than the children of men (Ps 44:3), became, for your salvation, the lowest of men, was despised, struck, scourged untold times throughout his entire body, and then died amid the suffering of the Cross.
> O most noble Queen,
> gaze upon [Him],
> consider [Him],
> contemplate [Him]
> as you desire to imitate [Him].[2]

The four words in this letter—gaze, consider, contemplate, imitate—reveal the whole dynamic of Franciscan prayer. These are the steps that guide the person toward transformation and intimate union.

Gaze: Gazing calls for a quiet attentiveness, simply being open to the wonderful presence of God with no words, no thoughts, just being there. The object of our gaze is the crucified Savior who stands before us as a mirror in which we see ourselves. To gaze involves desire, a response to the restless love that God has for us. To gaze is to have an openness to the Spirit of the Lord and an intent to strive for purity of heart. In Franciscan prayer the practice of gazing is critical. It is to pray long but with few words. Too many words, we know, can inhibit prayer. A simple story illustrates this point. A young girl was sitting quietly in church overcome with a sense of the presence and awesomeness of God. An adult enters and asks, "What are you doing?" The girl answers, "Nothing." The adult replies, "Say a Hail Mary then." The girl says the prayer, gets up and walks out. The words dissolved her spirit of prayer.

In the process of gazing, God awakens a hunger, a desire that yearns for more and more of the mystery we call God. In this penetrating gaze we get to the heart of reality as expressed in the following:

> When we gaze on this mirror of the cross we not only see who God is, self-giving love, but gazing on this God of humble love leads us to reflect on our own lives....The more we contemplate or dwell on the mystery of Christ by gazing upon the Crucified, the more we discover our own identity...and the more we will come to resemble Christ.[4]

For Francis and Clare this was the heart of reality, a pursuit that energized them for the whole of their lives.

Consider: The word consider encompasses the purity of one's focus. In the process of gazing one must center on the one essential thing, attempting to put aside anything that can alter or weaken one's gaze. It is to maintain a single-mindedness, a clear and straightforward focus. One's eyes are kept on Jesus alone. It is similar, perhaps, to the intimacy that two friends or two lovers share. Their focus is solely on each other, and as the image of the other becomes imprinted within, one begins to feel what the other feels. This is particularly true as one embraces the cross, which gives birth to compassion, the compassion Jesus modeled in his crucifixion. In this penetrating focus, one discovers God's love in Christ crucified. There is the enkindling of the flame of love in one's own heart. It behooves us to beg God each day to purify our focus, to center in on the one essential thing.

Contemplate: Contemplation requires a radical shift in thinking: Deep contemplative prayer is not so much learning how to contemplate God by some method or practice, as it is becoming aware that it is God who is contemplating us. Repeat this statement to yourself again and again: *Deep contemplative prayer is not so much learning how to contemplate God by some method or practice, as it is becoming aware that it is God who is contemplating us.* Prayer is too often viewed from a lopsided perspective, as something we must do, an obligation to fulfill or an effort on our part to reach out and try to contact a God "out there somewhere." But this is not prayer because there is no relationship, no intimacy of heart and spirit with this kind of separation. Thus one definition of prayer might be: Prayer is God praying in us. The God who lives in you and me prays in you and me. This frees us and is so right because it allows God to be God. Contemplation is not what I do, or what I do to God. It is what God does to me through an invitation to intimacy and union.

What a difference this could make if our prayer would begin with an awareness of this truth. It is true that we want to be with God, but all prayer begins because God wants us! We share with God, say our prayer words, express our needs and the needs of others. But we also have to respect God's perspective; we have to be attentive to God's touch and inspiration. This approach to prayer frees us from the compulsion that somehow we have to make prayer happen. It brings in a simplicity to prayer. God is always offering this invitation to us, but we are so reluctant to let go of our cherished, even boring, ways of prayer. We hang on, it seems, because if we do prayer the way we want, and perform all these exercises, then we can feel safe and in control of prayer, and in effect in control of God. When praying in this manner, we don't have to trust or step out in faith.

There is the story of a rooster who thought his crowing made the sun rise and that if he didn't crow, there would be no sun. But it is the sun that wakes up the rooster and makes him come alive. Likewise with God. We do not make God be. God makes us be. It is God who awakens life and power and insight in us because God contemplates us, loves us, prays within us.

Granting this basic premise that God prays within us, from our perspective, then, to pray is to listen, to be open, quiet and become attentive to the promptings of God's Spirit within. Here is where the first two steps in Clare's vision become so important. We gaze; we consider. Then we are drawn into contemplation all of which leads to imitation or transformation.

Imitate: To imitate does not mean to mimic the behavior of another. When Clare used the term, she was asking Agnes to become the image of the God on whom she gazed. To gaze, consider and contemplate Christ Crucified in the movement described above leads to transformation. What God has wanted me to be from all eternity, who I am to be in my inmost self, is imaged in God's Son hanging on the cross. When I gaze at the cross, I am looking into a mirror. I see my true self. What I take in Jesus' humility, poverty and charity, the characteristics of the self that make up who I am. Imitation is transformation insofar as Christ comes alive in my life. In this transformation contemplative union happens.

If we persist in doing prayer "my way," we remain on the insecure and unsteady ground of needing to control God. This kind of prayer tries to change the God to whom one is praying. If we recall ancient pagan rites, there was often the offering of a sacrifice to appease and awaken an indifferent god, or change the god's anger, or beg the god to protect the army. In contemporary times this would be like asking God to give victory to one's favorite football team. I wonder how often we might be tempted to pray in this manner. We try to pacify an angry God or make it up to God for our mistakes; we call upon God to change the weather or do things the way we think they should be. Or if we say enough prayers, maybe God will finally hear us. I often think of what Jesus said: "When you are praying, do not heap up empty phrases as the Gentiles do; for they think that they will be heard because of their many words" (Matthew 6:7). This is what happens when our image of God is "someone out there," apart from me.

Genuine prayer, or contemplation, is all about relationship. It is the kind of prayer in which God changes us over the course of time. It is the kind of prayer that allows God to enter in and become personally present to us. It is the prayer that allows God to pray within us so as to draw out what is best in us and speak to us in loving, personal terms, so that we go away from prayer a *transformed* person and we discover in ourselves the image God has always wanted us to be. Thus as we give ourselves over to the truth of "God contemplating me," God's gaze of love over the course of years transforms me, empowers me. In doing so, God slowly recognizes his own image in me. It is important to think of this in terms of relationships and the whole mystery of growing in love. I personally am not sure anyone can truly pray without being in love.

When we look at prayer this way we become not only transformed but empowered, and being so empowered, we are able to work to effect the necessary changes in life and society. God works in union with us, in union with our spirit, not apart from us. It is not a matter of God doing God's part according to our directions, and we doing ours apart from God. It is a matter of working at life together. I sometimes think of the scene in Exodus 3 when Moses sees a burning bush and encounters God. God gives Moses a mission to return to Egypt and liberate God's people. Moses wants nothing to do with this call and tries to get out of it. Then God says, "I will be with you" (Exodus 3:12). God did not say, "I will do it for you." God empowered Moses, and God does the same to us as we allow God to contemplate us. Wasn't this Francis' and Clare's goal in life? When Clare wrote gaze, consider, contemplate, imitate, it was precisely this kind of transformation and empowerment she (and Francis) had in mind.

Whoever is blessed with the opportunity to visit Assisi must spend time at the sanctuary of San Damiano. Go to the church restored by Francis and lived in by Clare. Sit before the main crucifix and allow the power of the place to take hold. Let yourself gaze, consider, contemplate and become transformed, at least a little, into the one on whom you are gazing.

Mary
Porziuncola

Francis' devotion to Mary is well-known. Of the churches he repaired during the early years of his conversion, his favorite was the one dedicated to Our Lady of the Angels. Thomas of Celano talks of Francis' affection:

> From there he moved to another place, which is called the "Portiuncula," where there stood a church of the Blessed Virgin Mother of God built in ancient times. At that time it was deserted and no one was taking care of it. When the holy man of God saw it so ruined, he was moved by piety because he had a warm devotion to the Mother of all good and he began to stay there continually. The restoration of that church took place in the third year of his conversion.[1]

The foundation of Francis' devotion to Mary was the fact that Mary was the Mother of our Lord Jesus. It was she who made the Lord of majesty our brother. The Scripture readings for the Feast of St. Mary of the Angels, August 2, support this view. In the reading from Galatians 4:3–7, Paul says, "God sent his Son, born of a woman...so that we might receive adoption as children." The Gospel passage from Luke 1:26ff. has Gabriel say to Mary, "And now, you will conceive in your womb and bear a son, and you will name him Jesus.... The Holy Spirit will come upon you, and the power of the Most High will overshadow you; therefore the child to be born will be holy; he will be called Son of God."

Mary becomes the Mother of the Word, the Son of God. And because of that we become sons and daughters of God; we achieve our status as adopted children. The Porziuncola epitomized this mystery and this truth for Francis, and so his tremendous love for this place. But this also flowed from the central plan that the Incarnation of Christ had in Francis' spirituality. Francis was resisting certain heretics of his day (Albigensians) who denied the reality of the Incarnation and the humanity of Christ. They would reduce Mary's role to nothing. Francis' firm belief opposed that stance. Jesus was Son of God and Son of Mary, the woman God chose as the Mother by means of which the Word became flesh.

Because of this Francis embraced Mary with an indescribable love, and as Mary gave birth to Jesus, Francis gave birth to a brotherhood at this place named after the Virgin. Bonaventure says,

> This is the place
> where the Order of Lesser Brothers
> was begun by St. Francis
> under the prompting of divine revelation.[2]

Though Francis was devoted to Mary as the Mother of Christ, his devotion was not overly sentimental, nor did he place her on a pedestal. There is a marvelous sentence in Francis' *Later Exhortation* that shows the true character of Francis' Marian spirituality. He writes, "We are...[Christ's] mothers when we carry Him in our heart and body through love and a pure and sincere conscience; and give Him birth through a holy activity, which must shine before others by example."[3]

Francis recognized that there are two moments in our life with God. There is the moment when we are passive, when God's grace overwhelms us, when we are forgiven, when we receive our new life in Christ. At this moment God is active; God does for us what we could never do for ourselves. But there is another moment when we become active, when we respond to God's grace, when we become sources of blessing in the lives of others, when we share the new life we have received, namely, Christ. We are then the Mothers of Christ. We receive Christ as Mary did, by God's grace, but then like Mary we are to bring Christ forth, to present Christ to a world in need.

Francis' Marian spirituality was not limited to singing Mary's praises. It moved Francis to action, to share with those in need. Further, the external sign of Francis' devotion to Mary was not the churches he built, or images before whom he prayed, or pilgrimages to Marian shrines, or prayers he said. The external sign of his devotion to Mary was Francis' determination to share her poverty.

There is a story from Thomas of Celano that illustrates this quite plainly:

> Brother Peter of Catanio, the saint's vicar, saw that great crowds of brothers from other places visited Saint Mary of the Portiuncula, and that the alms received were not sufficient to provide for their needs. He told Saint Francis: "Brother, *I don't know what to do;* I don't have enough to provide for all the crowds of brothers pouring in from all over. I beg you, please allow some of the goods of those entering as novices to be kept so that we can have recourse to these for expenses *in due season.*" But the saint replied, "May that piety be elsewhere, my dear brother, which treats the Rule with impiety for the sake of anyone." "Then, what should I do?" asked Peter. "Strip the Virgin's altar and take its adornments when you can't care for the needy in any other way. Believe me, she would be happier to have her altar stripped and the Gospel of her Son kept than have her altar decorated and her Son despised. The Lord will send someone to return to his Mother what He has loaned to us."[4]

The Marian spirituality of Francis moved him to become a source of blessing to others as Mary did. Mary presented the world its Savior.

Francis did all that he could to do the same. Because Mary shared the poverty and humility of Christ, so did Francis.

We too can honor Mary not by placing her on a pedestal but by sharing her poverty and presenting Christ to the world as she did. Our shrines to Mary ought to be the shelters for the homeless who share her poverty. Our words in praise of Mary ought to be the words and deeds we say and do to bring an end to war and terrorism in the name of the Queen of Peace. Our pilgrimages in her honor might be a walk for the poor. And although Francis' words about Mary are steeped in the sentiment characteristic of the church of his day, his piety went far beyond mere sentiment.

In order to be mothers of the Word and embrace the poverty and humility of Mary and her Son, Francis also found it important to pray like Mary. There is a place in Christian spirituality for praying to Mary, whether in word or in song. When, however, we explore Francis' devotion to Mary, it seems that he wanted, more than anything, to pray *like* Mary. Her example of the praying woman is exceptional and one might take that as a model for prayer.

How did Mary pray? The answer to this question comes from the Scriptures, particularly the first two chapters of the Gospel of Luke. After Gabriel came to Mary, Luke tells us in 1:29 that "she was much perplexed by his words and pondered what sort of greeting this might be." Then Mary added, "Here I am, the servant of the Lord; let it be with me according to your word" (1:38). After the shepherds left the child in the stable at Bethlehem "Mary treasured all these words and pondered them in her heart" (2:19). After Mary and Joseph found Jesus in the temple, "...they did not understand what he said to them. He went down with them and came to Nazareth, and was obedient to them; and his mother kept all these things in her heart."

The way to allow the Spirit of God to pray within us and speak of God's love is to ponder, like Mary, to question, to search, like Mary, to reflect and wonder, to humbly stand in openness, listening and reflecting on the mystery, gazing on the wonder that came into her life. If I pray *like* Mary, then the same things that happened to Mary can happen to me: Jesus is conceived within me, the Word becomes flesh, I become "full of grace," the will of God happens, I give birth to the Lord, and I am blessed.

What attracted Francis to Mary most of all was her motherhood. She was Mother of the Word, Mother of the Son of God; she gave birth to the Word and therefore our brother. And so Francis could encourage us in turn to be mothers of the Word, to give birth to Jesus in our lives. We could come to know this by praying as Mary did.

Francis loved St. Mary of the Angels more than any other place in the world. He told his friars never to abandon that church. It was here that his life with God began, here it was nurtured and here he spent his last moments when he died. He entrusted this place to his brothers at his death as the most beloved of the Virgin.

As a pilgrim in Assisi, take the local bus to St. Mary of the Angels in the valley below. Humbly and gratefully enter the main basilica and the tiny chapel, the Porziuncola, under the cupola, the one dedicated to Mary, the one Francis himself restored. Feel the stones, many of which were put in by his hands. Drink in the spirit of Mary and the Spirit of God. Quietly ponder, listen, gaze and reflect on the love of God that is so real and tangible in this holy place. And allow yourself to sense the Word of God taking flesh within you.

Commitment and Fidelity
San Paolo in Bastia

Bastia is important in the Franciscan story because of Clare's presence there, even if only for a brief period. After Clare left her paternal home on Palm Sunday night in 1212 and joined Francis and the brothers at the Porziuncola in the valley below Assisi, Francis had to decide where to take Clare. She could not stay with the brothers. So he and a few companions journeyed with her to the Benedictine monastery of San Paolo in the nearby locale of Bastia, about two or three miles away.

This area is now the cemetery for the local inhabitants of Bastia and all that remains is the original chapel that was used by the sisters. That chapel becomes a place of significance in the Franciscan story because of what happened shortly after Clare arrived. When Clare's family realized what she had done, her uncle Monaldo and a few other knights came charging down the hillside of Assisi into the monastery complex with the intent of bringing Clare back home. Clare, however, took sanctuary in the chapel of the nuns, and while clinging to the altar, displayed her shorn hair and claimed her new life in religion. That altar is still present and is a moving testimony to the strength and power of Clare's commitment.

Part of the account in the Process of Canonization of Saint Clare relates:

> Then St. Francis gave her the tonsure before the altar in the church of the Virgin Mary, called the Portiuncula, and then sent her to the church of San Paolo delle Abbadesse. When her relatives wanted to drag her out, Lady Clare grabbed the altar cloths and uncovered her head, showing them she was tonsured. In no way did she acquiesce, neither letting them take her from the place nor remaining with them.[1]

The Legend of Saint Clare is more descriptive:

After the news reached her relatives...they ran to the place...employed violent force, poisonous advice, and flattering promises, persuading her to give up such a worthless deed that was unbecoming to her class and without precedence in her family. But, taking hold of the altar cloths, she bared her tonsured head, maintaining that she would in no way be torn away from the service of Christ.

With the increasing violence of her relatives, her spirit grew, and her love—provoked by injuries—provided strength. So, for many days, even though she endured an obstacle in the way of the Lord and her own [relatives] opposed her proposal of holiness, her spirit did not crumble and her fervor did not diminish. Instead, amid words and deeds of hatred, she molded her spirit anew in hope until her relatives, turning back, were quiet.[2]

Clare's experience at San Paolo in Bastia invites us to reflect on the meaning of fidelity to a commitment, whether it be marriage vows, religious vows, friendship, a life of prayer or commitment to a worthy cause. Lifelong fidelity has often been questioned. Some philosophies of life proclaim that to be wholly human, a person need not feel obliged to remain faithful to previous decisions should something new and better come along. This became evident to me one day when I was interviewing a young man who had requested approval for permanent profession in religious life. In such interviews I always asked about permanency of commitment. He answered that he could say yes to his vows, but if something better, or different, came his way in five years, he would consider pursuing that. I was grateful for his honesty, but somewhat stunned by his mentality.

Such a stance in life leads to what Karl Rahner called an "interior discontinuity." The inside of the person remains forever unsettled, scattered, broken up. There is not the opportunity for a developmental, deepening process of life. And this can lead to halfheartedness or a part-time heartedness toward anything or anyone. One's energies are without focus.

The experience of fidelity, especially lifelong fidelity to a commitment, makes greater integrity in life and deeper inner harmony possible. Even though other options or choices can be made, the experience of fidelity leads to an *inner continuity* in my being. I feel something whole in my heart. I begin to know something new inside. For example, remaining faithful to God in prayer over a lifetime when it is legitimate to make other choices—like needed sleep or the demands of work; remaining faithful to one's spouse when 80 or 90 percent of life can be so ordinary and routine and divorce is an easy option; remaining faithful to one's religious vows when the secular world constantly presents other inviting options. Those who choose fidelity speak of a depth and growth others might miss and often experience a kind of life others do not understand.

Gabriel Marcel, a French philosopher, refers to this in offering one of the finest proofs for the existence of God, which he based on the reality of love. True and genuine love, he claimed, is the greatest proof of eternity. When a person says, "I love you" to another, it has to imply forever. In other words, in saying, "I love you," the intent is never, "I love you this week, or this month, but I'm not so sure about next week." When I gaze into someone's eyes and declare my love with the whole of my heart, it has to mean "forever." I also choose the consequences of that declaration. I commit myself to the consequences of that act, not knowing ahead of time what those consequences might be. I choose to say "yes" to the consequences even before they happen, which means I will say "yes" over and over again throughout a whole lifetime. This is real freedom.

We learn from the example of Mary, our Blessed Mother. Mary did only one thing with her life; she conceived her son. Everything else was simply an unfolding of this single theme of her life. She did not merely say "yes" once, in some great moment; she sustained that yes patiently, silently, constantly, in the serene assurance of the true believer, in a mature simplicity that brought greatness, without regret. Francis and Clare reflect this single heartedness and steadfastness by which they lived out their original yes and inspiration over a lifetime, even in the face of opposition from brothers or family members or the church. These are examples of an inner continuity that brought freedom and fullness of life.

What makes it possible to remain faithful? Primarily it is grace and the experience of God's fidelity to us. God has made a covenant with each of us and God is faithful. We must believe this. We also get strength and insight from human relationships. The healthier our relationships are, the more the experience of fidelity becomes reinforced and real. We sense what it means to respond with a whole heart. And as we experience fidelity from others, we are given the strength to grow in fidelity ourselves.

A pilgrim can spend many days in Assisi. If so, hire a taxi and go to the cemetery in Bastia. It is a ten- to fifteen-minute ride. Enter the ancient chapel. Sit in quiet prayer or read from the life of Clare and gaze at the altar. It is the altar to which she clung when her relatives tried to force her to abandon the path of the gospel she had chosen. In our Franciscan Study Pilgrimages we make a visit with the entire group. When Poor Clares are in the group, we ritualize the experience Clare had in 1212. Clinging to that same altar the Poor Clares renew their commitment and fidelity to the gospel. It is always a moving and touching moment.

[23]

Fascination With God and Freedom
Lago Trasimeno

There is an intriguing story about how Saint Francis spent Lent of the year 1213. It appears in *The Little Flowers of Saint Francis*.

Once Saint Francis was alongside the Lake of Perugia [Trasimeno] on the day of Carnival, at the house of a man devoted to him, where he was lodged for the night. He was inspired by God to go to make that Lent on an island in the lake. So Saint Francis asked this devout man that, for love of Christ, he carry him with his little boat to an island of the lake where no one lived, and that he do this on the night of the Day of the Ashes, so that no one would notice. And this man, out of love—from the great devotion he had for Saint Francis—promptly fulfilled his request and carried him to that island. And Saint Francis took nothing with him except two small loaves of bread....

Since there was no dwelling in which he could take shelter, he went into some very thick brush that was formed like a little den or a little hut by many bushes and saplings. And in this place he put himself in prayer and contemplation of heavenly things. And there he stayed the whole of Lent without eating or drinking, except for half of one of those little loaves, as his devoted friend found on Holy Thursday when he returned for him; for of the two loaves he found one whole one and a half; the other half, it is supposed, Saint Francis ate, out of reverence for the fast of the blessed Christ, who fasted for forty days and forty nights without taking any material food.[1]

This event reveals a wonderful quality about Francis' freedom of spirit. When Jesus was in the desert for forty days, he had no synagogue for the Sabbath. He simply wished to keep his gaze on the

Father. When Francis spent time on the island (called Isola Maggiore) for forty days, he had no church, no priest for Sunday Mass. He came here with two loaves of bread and a desire to imitate Jesus, his Lord, by spending time in fasting and prayer just as Jesus did.

In this context a good definition for penance could be fascination with God, an absorption in God, not a fascination with mortification or penitential practices. The island is a place where Francis spent time deepening his fascination with great freedom of spirit. No methods, no formal practices. Simply a heart directed to God.

When we come to a moment in life of desiring fuller conversion, we are in effect becoming aware that God is asking for more. One's heart might sense this tug, feel the call to respond with more of whatever it might be. Not more legalism or more mortification, but more interior holiness, more development into the likeness of God. This is what is meant by a summons to penance, a summons to a turning of one's heart. This summons is a grace, a gift freely given. We do not achieve it or make it happen. Rather, God converts us and empowers us to respond with more of our hearts. Francis himself realized that prayer or fasting cannot change one's heart. Only God can.

I am reminded of a Scripture text from Hosea 6:6, "For I desire steadfast love and not sacrifice, / the knowledge of God rather than burnt offerings." And in Matthew 9:13 Jesus says, "Go and learn what this means, 'I desire mercy, not sacrifice.' For I have come to call not the righteous but sinners."

There is mystery in this. In the religious dimension of life, or that facet we call "religion," we spend so much energy trying to earn our place with God or gain God's favor. We can easily get caught in a web of legalities or a penchant for fulfilling all kinds of obligations.

Surely the church's laws that guide us, and the obligations to which we need to pay attention, have their place and are important. The wisdom of the Scriptures, however, reminds us that more than anything we need to keep a heart focused on the living God and to strive for purity of heart. This was central to Francis' spirituality.

God wants our hearts, not our sacrifices. Isn't that hard to swallow? God wants us to spend a lifetime nurturing a heart turned toward the Lord. God wants a spirit that knows it is free to love and show mercy. It all depends on how our hearts are centered. If the very center of our life turns to God, then the rest of us will do the same. Our concern will not be the fulfillment of prescriptions or legalities, but the direction and the movement of our hearts.

Often we have a sense that our hearts are in the right place and are turning to God when we welcome outcasts, when we offer mercy and show compassion, when we spontaneously respond to those in need, when we generously give of time and resources with no thought of the cost, when we eat with "sinners and tax collectors." These latter are those we find unacceptable in the family, or community, someone with whom we are angry; or maybe we are the sinner because another is justifiably angry with us.

In writing to a Poor Clare, Saint Bonaventure said, "Your heart is to be an altar of God. It is here that the fire of intense love must burn always."[2] If this is true then the first church is in the human heart. There is no sense going to church (a building) for prayer if one has not entered into the church (dwelling place) of one's heart.

This is what Francis did at Trasimeno. He entered the church of his heart. He made of his heart an altar for God. His choice to spend Lent on an island was not of his doing or of some pious romantic fling. He was captured, seized, by the Spirit of God. And when God grasps us in the heart, the deepest center of our lives, then we can let go and we are moved to adoration. Then we realize the meaning of the words of Scripture, "For I desire steadfast love and not sacrifice, the knowledge of God rather than burnt offerings."

In our work with pilgrim groups in Assisi we often make a day's excursion to Lago Trasimeno, about an hour's ride from Assisi. The ferryboat crossing out to the island where Francis spent an entire Lent takes thirty minutes. In a ritual prayer each person is given two small loaves of bread and is asked to fast for much of the day with only those two loaves. With song and reading we pray over each one, "May our Lord Jesus Christ, symbolized by this bread, be your food for the journey into life." If you ever have an opportunity to visit this holy place, take along the reading from *The Little Flowers of Saint Francis*, or the Scriptures, and two small loaves of bread with a half-liter of water. Walk around the island; walk to the spot where Francis disembarked when he arrived there in 1213. Go with the desire to nurture a fascination with God, with no other focus except a heart that wants more and more of the mystery of God. Today there are about sixty inhabitants on the island, but much of it is wilderness and lends itself to solitude and prayer.

On Being Subject to Every Human Creature
Porziuncola

As the heart and center of Francis' life, the Porziuncola was also the heart of a "mission consciousness," a spirit of evangelization from its earliest days. From here the brothers were sent out to preach. They returned here to share their faith and experiences and to be nourished by one another.

One factor that contributed to this sense of mission was the very physical setting of the Porziuncola. It was outside the city, in the woods, and among the outcasts. In their dramatization of the Gospel, the brothers rewrote the script of life that included: the primacy of God, a spirit of prayer and penance, a life of simplicity and poverty, ministry to lepers (the outsiders), brothers from every walk of life or social status living together, living among the little people, the poor, working with their hands and caring for the needy, being messengers of peace and reconciliation and doing all this within the church. From this new style of life, the Good News of the gospel was once again made visible. This shocked the people and made them wonder.

The brothers did not stay around Assisi but quickly branched out from St. Mary's to nearby villages and towns. Thomas of Celano describes it well:

> At that same time, another good man entered their religion, and they increased their number to eight. Then the blessed Francis called them all to himself and told them many things about *the kingdom of God*, contempt of the world, denial of their own will, and subjection of the body. He separated them in four groups of two each.
>
> "Go, my dear brothers," he said to them, "*two by two* through different parts of the world, *announcing peace* to the people and *penance for the remission of sins*. Be *patient in trials*, confident that the Lord will fulfill His plan and promise.

Respond humbly to those who question you. *Bless those who persecute you.* Give thanks to those who harm you and bring false charges against you, for because of these things an *eternal kingdom is prepared* for us."[1]

After their initial Rule was confirmed by Innocent III in 1209, more brothers came, so they were again divided into pairs and sent forth. In the regular meetings or chapters held at the Porziuncola, a major issue always had to do with mission, with expansion and preaching. By 1212 missions to foreign and hostile nations began. As the brothers traveled to countries and provinces outside Italy, it was with a lifestyle and witness similar to the example set at the Porziuncola.

Following the chapter in May 1219, the decision was made to send expeditions all over the world: Germany, France, Spain, England and eventually all corners of the globe. Francis himself set out in 1219 to work among the Saracens. He arrived in Damietta, Egypt, on August 29 of that year. Thomas of Celano writes:

Taking a companion with him, he was not afraid to present himself to the sight of the Sultan of the Saracens....

Before he reached the Sultan, he was captured by soldiers, insulted and beaten, but was not afraid. He did not flinch at threats of torture nor was he shaken by death threats. Although he was ill-treated by many with a hostile spirit and a harsh attitude, he was received very graciously by the Sultan. The Sultan honored him as much as he could, offering him many gifts, trying to turn his mind to worldly riches. But when he saw that he resolutely scorned all these things like dung, the Sultan was overflowing with admiration and recognized him as a man unlike any other. He was moved by his words and *listened to him very willingly.*[2]

Francis' experience among the Saracens led him to a new understanding of evangelization and gave him a revolutionary insight on
how to evangelize. This is captured in chapter sixteen of the Rule of
1221, entitled: "Those Going Among the Saracens and Other
Nonbelievers." Francis writes:

> As for the brothers who go, they can live spiritually among the
> Saracens and nonbelievers in two ways. One way is not to
> engage in arguments or disputes but to be subject *to every*
> *human creature for God's sake* and to acknowledge that they are
> Christians. The other way is to announce the Word of God,
> when they see it pleases the Lord....[3]

The key phrase here, which also captures a major principle of
Francis' spirituality, is the statement: Let them "be subject to every
human creature for God's sake." It appears that Francis was recon-
sidering his own missionary behavior. At first his was a desire for
martyrdom. Now his primary focus is Islam and how to live among
its followers. The idea was to live not separately in a Christian
colony, but among the Muslims. Francis himself received safe conduct from the Sultan to go, live and travel among his people. In
telling his brothers, above all, to be subject to every human creature
for God's sake, because they are Christian, his aim was a quality of
religious presence. Francis never acted like a "knight" or "cru-
sader" for the faith, which was the great rage of his day. He never
sent his brothers as preachers of the crusade or to promote it.
Neither did he act with superiority to the "unbeliever." Everything
came from the grace of God and if the "unbeliever" had the same
grace as Francis he would have been more grateful. Never did any
word or allusion offensive to Islam appear in his writings, a rarity in
his day, even among saints.

For us, the secret to this type of presence as a means of evange-lization is that we are there, among others, to receive from their richness, rather than trying to change them or give them some-thing. A document written in 1983 stated:

> The great majority of people in the world are non-Christian. We must recognize the other living faiths (Buddhism, Islam, Hinduism, etc.) as gifts of God and deal with their people as our brothers and sisters. We should try to initiate a dialogue of life with them. By establishing com-munities of presence among them, we can receive of their insights into the mystery of God, while we await God's action in them.[4]

It takes humility, a spirit of minority, to be able to do this. To work among people with the intention that "I am going to bring you something" as though what they already have is not of much value, often implies control or power. To "give" in that sense reflects a spirit of domination, which is destructive of evangelization.

What Francis taught, that which was born at the Porziuncola as the brothers began to make an impact on local Assisians and even-tually the world, was that one must allow oneself to receive the gift of what other cultures and peoples have, the gifts of love and life and sharing, the gifts of faith and trust, the gift and presence of God in them without submitting to that compulsion which claims, "What I have is better."

We all believe we have the ability to give—love, friendship, the Good News. But the ability to receive the treasure buried in the heart of another who looks and thinks and believes differently than I do is quite something else. We have to call forth the Good News inside another by humbly coming before that person in our weakness and receiving the treasure of life, the beauty of God's gift that is there.

One of the rituals we often use at the Porziuncola is called the "Ritual of Sending Out." It is a simple service of prayer that recalls Francis' sending out the brothers two by two. We call pilgrims forth in groups of two or four to send them forth into the rest of their lives as mothers and fathers, husbands and wives, pastors and preachers, teachers and ministers. We call pilgrims forth to live out the gospel, to witness the Good News, and to do so in the spirit of Francis. We offer encouragement, to be men and women of peace, patience and thankfulness.

The spirituality one might take from a visit to St. Mary of the Angels is precisely to put on the spirit with which Francis sent out the first brothers, especially to be "subject to every human creature for God's sake," and to "Cast all your anxiety on him, because he cares for you" (1 Peter 5:7). This is the spirit that must guide one's ministry and that gives our work a Franciscan face.

25

Franciscan Rule of Life
Fonte Colombo

The sanctuary of Fonte Colombo in the Rieti Valley, Francis' second home, is the place where Francis finalized his Rule of Life for the friars. Although this Rule was for the members of the First Order, the place gives us an opportunity to consider how fidelity to any one of the Franciscan Rules fulfills the longing of every human heart.

Whatever Franciscan Rule of Life one may follow, First Order, Second Order, Third Order Regular or Third Order Secular, the basis for every one of these is the same, summed up in Francis' words in his *Testament*, "The Most High Himself revealed to me that I should live according to the pattern of the Holy Gospel."[1] For each of the different branches the Rule grew into a "form of life" based on the gospel.

Even though we can trace the development over time of Francis' Rule, for him there always existed only one Rule, that of the gospel life which was always in process. It was a "Rule on the move," characterized by walking in the footprints of Jesus Christ. The development of the Rule for all the families of the Franciscan movement was similar. All were expressions of the same divine inspiration that evolved over time and was formed by the lived experience of the sisters and brothers, according to the teaching of the church and Francis' vision.

A wonderful experience is to have copies of the four Franciscan Rules, representing the four Franciscan families. Every Rule begins with the same words.

• First Order Friars—"The Rule and Life of the Lesser Brothers is this: to observe the Holy Gospel of Our Lord Jesus Christ."
• Second Order Poor Clares—"The form of life of the Order of the Poor Sisters that blessed Francis established is this: to observe the Holy Gospel of Our Lord Jesus Christ."
• Third Order Regular—"The form of life of the Brothers and Sisters

is this: to observe the Holy Gospel of Our Lord Jesus Christ,"

• Third Order Secular—"The rule and life of the Secular Franciscans is this: to observe the gospel of Our Lord Jesus Christ by following the example of Saint Francis of Assisi."

Commitment to a Rule, whether for religious or seculars, is a response to a call and to one of the deepest longings of the heart, namely, the authentic desire for union with God. Fonte Colombo inspires us to ask how this comes about. The answer lies in fidelity to the mission of life, the mission of living one's Rule. Some examples might help.

In Genesis 12 God called Abraham and gave him a mission. The call however was not his moment of union with God. Rather the experience of union and intimacy happened years later after he was faithful to the mission God gave. It was then that Abraham experienced a covenant with God through which God drew Abraham into intimacy (see Genesis 17).

In Exodus 3 Moses received a call through the burning bush, a unique event and surely a sign of special union. Yet the real moments of encounter with God were not at the call on Mount Horeb but at the end of his life as seen in Exodus 33, which described Moses' intimacy and friendship with God. This was the consequence of having been faithful to the lifelong mission God had given him.

For Saint Paul, the real marvel in his life was not in the descriptive event of his conversion when he met Jesus. Rather the strength and power of Paul's preaching came from his lifelong fidelity to the mission given to him by Christ, captured perhaps in the words, "[I]t is no longer I who live, but it is Christ who lives in me" (Galatians 2:20).

At Fonte Colombo, through many days of prayer and fasting in the early fall of 1223, Francis reflected on a lifetime of God's fidelity to him and his fidelity to his mission to live the gospel life completely.

Most Franciscan pilgrimages include a visit to Fonte Colombo. While there, one can walk down the side of the mountain to the cave where Francis prayed and fasted, where together with some of the brothers he put together a final draft of the Franciscan Rule of Life. There is a tiny chapel above the cave dedicated to the Archangel Michael. One might wish to spend some time in that chapel. If you are a Franciscan, perhaps you might consider renewing your commitment to your particular Franciscan Rule of Life. If you are not a Franciscan, but Christian, you might consider renewing your commitment to the gospel way of life. If you are Muslim or Jewish, perhaps you would be inspired to renew your dedication to the living God through the Torah or the Qur'an. The focus would be to make clear, and deepen, one's fidelity to the call of life, the call of God, and to bring to mind with a grateful heart how one's union with God has matured over a lifetime of fidelity.

When Francis heard the Gospel on February 24, 1208, and understood what the Gospel was calling forth from him, he exclaimed, "This is what I want; this is what I desire; this is what I long to do with all my heart."[2] A lifetime of responding to that call resulted in an intimacy and union with God, an awareness of which can still leave one breathless.

26

The Feast of Feasts
Greccio

Christmas was Francis' favorite feast. It was for him the Feast of Feasts, and he wanted to celebrate it in a special way. Why? Because the all Good God chose to be born in human flesh. Because the Word was conceived in the womb of the Virgin. Because our all Good God was born each day in the eucharistic bread of the altar. But most of all because of God's *great love*, revealed to us in the Incarnation. For Francis the way this love was being celebrated at Christmas fell short. He felt that the traditional liturgical celebration of the time failed to awaken and touch hearts.

So what did Francis do? It was December of 1223. Francis had recently returned from Rome where Pope Honorius III approved his Rule of Life, November 29, 1223. Celano and Bonaventure described what happened and the preparation that took place about fifteen days before the feast of Christmas near the little village of Greccio in the Rieti Valley. This is Celano's account:

> We should note then, as a matter worthy of memory and something to be recalled with reverence, what he did, three years prior to his death, at the town of Greccio, on the birth-day of our Lord Jesus Christ. *There was a certain man in that area* named John who *had a good reputation* and an even better manner of life. Blessed Francis loved him with special affection....Blessed Francis had John summoned to him some fifteen days prior to the birthday of the Lord. "If you desire to celebrate the coming feast of the Lord together at Greccio," he said to him, "hurry before me and carefully make ready the things I tell you. For I wish to enact the memory of that babe who was born in Bethlehem: to see as much as is possible with my own bodily eyes the discomfort of his infant needs, how he lay in a manger, and how, with an ox and an ass standing by, he rested on hay." Once the good and faithful man had heard

Francis' words, he ran quickly and prepared in that place all the things that the holy man had requested.[1]

In this dramatic reenactment of the events of Bethlehem, Francis wished to recall the simplicity and poverty, the inconveniences and humility of the Christ Child's birth.

Most of all he wanted to celebrate the mystery of God's great love, a love that God made concrete in a little child wrapped in swaddling clothes, a love that had the power to remake the world, a love that invited one to become a new creature, a love that invited people to believe in the impossible, a love that asked all to forget their sin and darkness and trust God's goodness. This love was reenacted by Francis through the visual picture of Bethlehem placed before the eyes of the people in Greccio's cave.

One of Francis' and the friars' greatest difficulties with the renewing of the church was that the people they were addressing were already Christians. The people knew the basic stories and teaching, as we do. They had seen other visual images of the nativity. But their hearts needed to be reached again. How does one preach the Word of God to those who think that they already understand it? How does one listen and feel as if though one were hearing and witnessing the stories of the Gospels for a first time? How did Francis reach people with a message they have heard again and again? He decided to concretize God's great love through a visual picture of Bethlehem, placing it before the eyes of the people.

At Midnight Mass, Francis used words in his sermon, but he also made the Incarnation real and immediate through props: an ox, an ass, a manger, a cave, singing and the warmth of love. The setting helped people not only celebrate an event that happened twelve hundred years before, but it also helped to open their hearts to God's love and the coming of Christ into them again. Greccio was made, as it were, a new Bethlehem.

Bonaventure says,

Francis' example,
when considered by the world,
is capable of arousing
the hearts of those who are sluggish in the faith of Christ.[2]

The faith had grown cold. Celano describes a vision of John of Velita, "For the man saw a little child lying lifeless in the manger and he saw the holy man of God approach the child and waken him from a deep sleep. Nor is this vision unfitting, since in the hearts of many the child Jesus has been given *over to oblivion*. Now he is awakened and impressed on their loving memory by His own grace through His holy servant Francis."[3]

Francis also had an altar placed over the manger because he wanted to show the connection between the coming of Jesus in the flesh in the manger and the sacramental coming of Jesus on the eucharistic altar. A lifeless baby appeared in the manger and when Francis reached down to pick it up, the baby came alive in the arms of Francis. This was symbolic of Christ coming to life in the hands of the priest at the altar. Scholars point out that this is a most appropriate interpretation for the event that happened at Greccio: the manifestation of the human birth of Jesus in the manger and his sacramental birth each day upon the altar.

Francis' focus on Christmas as the Feast of Feasts and the manifestation of God's love gave birth to a new understanding of the Incarnation. Most of us have learned that God sent his Son to be born as one like us to make right the first sin of Adam and Eve. So without sin there would have been no need for the Incarnation. Because of Francis, the Franciscans have developed an alternate interpretation. God's plan for having his Son become one like us was part of God's original design for all creation from the very beginning. It was not an afterthought on God's part, something God decided to do to make up for original sin and human sinfulness. God longed for all eternity to become human, and God's Son accomplished that through his birth at Bethlehem. The Incarnation of the Son of God is the means by which God shares most fully his life and love for humanity, and the means by which human beings can share in divine life.

This can dramatically alter our image of God and the way we celebrate Christmas.

We learn from the great Franciscan theologian John Duns Scotus that the whole purpose of creation on God's part was to come to a point in time for the Incarnation of God's Son to take place as the most resplendent creative act of God. When God decided to create, the Incarnation had to be first and foremost in God's mind, and not dependent on any action of humans, especially sin. This was a natural outflow of love, and God, above all, wished to communicate to us the fullness of divine love. What better way than to send the Son.

This image helps us to appreciate the depth and beauty of our humanness. Our human nature is good. This also gives us a new and transformed image of God, not as someone who is vindictive and waiting to punish us for sin or someone who is constrained to react to our manipulations. The God we see in this image is a God of such overflowing love that it spills over into all of creation and into our hearts.

Francis obviously did not express these truths in his own words. The Greccio event, however, provided the impetus for a refreshing new way to understand the Incarnation. Francis intuited this majestic truth because he was so convinced of it through his experience of God's overwhelming love. There was no better moment of the year than Christmas to celebrate that love. And so Greccio happened.

The crib scene responded perfectly to the need humanity always has, and that the Middle Ages had with a particular intensity, namely to see visibly that which they believe. Francis undoubtedly gave new impetus to devotion to the humanity of Christ and impetus to devotion to the place of the Christmas crèche. It was the humility, simplicity and purity of the faith of Francis that made Greccio the prototype of the crib as we know it. To attribute the invention of the crib to Francis does not square away with history as archival documents portray. The merit of Francis has not been in inventing a Christmas setting that all can reproduce, but in having shown to all the kind of heart one must have to welcome the Child Jesus and thereby welcome God's great and tender love. God became a child, that we might have someone to love. Francis reenacted the Christmas story so that, again, the hearts of all might be roused knowing how much they are loved.

The sanctuary of Greccio is difficult to access, but it can be done. It is my hope that in your lifetime you may be blessed with an opportunity to journey up this mountain in the Rieti Valley that will take you to this holy place where, in one sense, Christmas is celebrated 365 days of the year. While there, read Luke's account of the birth of Jesus. Sing some Christmas carols, at least in your heart. Spend time in the cave chapel, called *Grotta del Presepio;* let the scene of Bethlehem rouse your heart to knowing that God loves you.

You are someone special to the Lord. You are someone God has called to a newness you cannot even imagine, a newness made visible and possible by the Incarnation of God's beloved Son.

During Advent time a frequent emotion is that of *waiting* for the Lord to come. I think, however, that it makes more sense to consider this sentiment from the opposite perspective. Namely, it is God who is waiting on us; it is God who is waiting on us to believe that we can become someone we have never yet been, and to believe that we truly are lovable and loved. After all, God has given us a babe in swaddling clothes to help us realize we need not be overwhelmed by what often seems to be a truth beyond our imagining.

27

The Power, Wisdom and
Beauty of the Cross
La Verna

La Verna is a mountain in the Tuscan region of central Italy. It is about eighty miles north of Assisi and is truly holy ground. In 1213 Count Orlando of Chiusi, a wealthy nobleman, donated the mountain to Francis and his brothers as a place suitable for prayer, penance, peace, rest and all things that might nourish the spirit. Arnaldo Fortini's descriptive account, however, would make one wonder how suitable a place La Verna was. He writes:

> La Verna. It is a mountain surmounted by an immense cliff, rising vertically, cut off from the rest of the mountain on all sides.... It is a mass of stone surmounted by furious storm clouds. A retreat for prayer in the harshness of winter. An altar in the heart of holy Italy, between its two seas, between the sources of two of its immortal rivers, whose waters have mirrored ages of iron and bronze. ...In vain one searches for the peace that Orlando had promised to Francis. The whole gigantic crag seems tormented, wounded, and broken in some horrendous convulsion. Violent passion made grievously immobile lurks in the fearsome rock that is constantly assaulted by storms, rock that seems of another world.... This fortress does not bring to mind angelic ecstasies. It is more a setting for a battle of titans. Covering the rocky rampart, which on all sides plunges downward in a straight line, are fearful bastions, enormous towers, inaccessible citadels, all made by the bedlam of twisted rock.[1]

On Francis' first visit to La Verna in 1213 he received a revelation about this mountain that contributes to the mysticism of this holy place. The description is similar to Fortini's account and relates well to Francis' experience in September of 1224, when he received the wounds of Christ on his flesh. The following comes from "The

Second Consideration of the Stigmata" found in *The Little Flowers of St. Francis*.

> A few days later St. Francis was standing beside that cell [that Orlando made for him], gazing at the form of the mountain and marveling at the great chasms and openings in the massive rocks. And he began to pray, and then it was revealed to him by God that those striking chasms had been made in a miraculous way at the hour of Christ's Passion when, as the Gospel says, "the rocks split." And God wanted this to be manifested in a special way here on Mount Alverna in order to show that the Passion of Christ was to be renewed on that mountain in the soul of St. Francis by love and compassion and in his body by the imprinting of the Stigmata.[2]

Some might consider these words as mere fiction, the creation of an imaginative thinker. Or, one might choose to accept them from a faith perspective. On visiting La Verna one can either walk down to the Sasso Spico (The Projecting Rock) below the main part of the sanctuary or climb to the top of the mountain. The impression one will have is exactly as that described above. The mountain truly seems torn apart by some massive convulsion, with rocks split and large crevices and dangerous caverns. Whatever approach one takes, it is important to allow oneself to experience the mountain, to enter into it spiritually and mystically.

There are many ways one can reflect on La Verna. Obviously this place emphasizes the centrality of the cross in Christian life. Perhaps it would be helpful for a person to consider ways in which he or she views the cross as one way of entering into the spirituality of this place.

Some look at the cross and see only suffering or principally suffering. Others gaze at the cross and think, "To become like Jesus means that I become one filled with suffering and pain." Thus, I want to avoid the cross at all costs. Still others look for suffering so as to become like Jesus.

At this point in my life all this appears a bit differently. In my own personal prayer space there hangs an image of the San Damiano crucifix. I gaze upon this cross every day, but as I look upon the cross I no longer see suffering; rather I see open-armed, unconditional, extravagant, self-giving love. I find myself confronted, and comforted, as I gaze on the cross, with the truth that this kind of love (which Jesus' open arms signify) is the only kind that can put hatred to rest, that can break the forces of violence and bring us comfort and strength in our sorrows, whether personally or between nations, or among families and societies. And even though like everyone else I have had my share of heartaches and pain, being hurt and feeling crushed, life is too rich and too short to permit the mystery of suffering to control me or force me to concentrate on that dimension alone.

Each year on September 14 we celebrate the Feast of the Triumph of the Cross. Each year during Holy Week we celebrate Good Friday, which liturgically is also a feast of triumph. The cross is a triumph because it symbolizes the reality that the power of love has broken, once and for all, the power of self-centeredness, sin and death. This power of love came through the cross, no other way. Consider for a moment how powerful hatred or revenge can be. The power of love, as modeled on the cross, triumphed over that.

This same power and triumph are ours. These are our tools for dealing with life. When facing something difficult, when crushed by pain and hurt, when one's heart is full of hatred, when all we can think of is revenge, retaliating or getting even, choose instead to sit, kneel or prostrate yourself before the cross, gaze on it and let its power and wisdom enter into you, transform you, transform your hatred, vengeance, anger, self-pity or bitterness so that you become like the one on whom you gaze. My experience is that this really works. If you do not want to believe it, at least try it.

I often think of Saint Paul's words:

> For the message about the cross is foolishness to those who are perishing, but to us who are being saved it is the power of God....
>
> For Jews demand signs and Greeks desire wisdom, but we proclaim Christ crucified, a stumbling-block to Jews and foolishness to Gentiles, but to those who are the called, both Jews and Greeks, Christ the power of God and the wisdom of God. For God's foolishness is wiser than human wisdom, and God's weakness is stronger than human strength. (1 Corinthians 1:18–19, 22–25)

As you gaze upon the cross, let your heart and mind know that you are gazing at the wisdom of God and the power of love. When you do that the focus goes off suffering and you see love at work, which was Jesus' entire goal. There is no weapon that can overcome the wisdom and love that comes through the cross.

The cross was central to the life of Francis and Clare. From the moment the image of Christ spoke to Francis from the crucifix at San Damiano until he was marked with the wounds of Jesus at La Verna, Celano tells us Francis burned with an unquenchable fire to know this Lord, to experience and know the wisdom that came from such love. Francis wanted not so much to know what this pain is, but what kind of love this is.

Clare would hear in her contemplation of the cross the invitation to be transformed. And so she would counsel Agnes: Gaze upon Christ, consider Christ, contemplate Christ, imitate Christ and become like the One upon whom you are gazing, not to look for suffering, crucifixion or pain, but to enflesh that same kind of open-armed, self-giving, unconditional love that Jesus' presence on the cross symbolizes. And to know that this is the only power that can transform the world and rebuild life.

This is what we are invited to taste, to welcome, to pursue: the open arms of Jesus on the cross, the open heart and life of Francis eager to embrace the cross, the open welcoming gaze of Clare onto the cross. Gaze, so as to taste. Taste, so as to become like the One on whom you gaze, that we might become the incarnation of God's unconditional love.

Scholars tell us there were three possible ways the Stigmata may have happened. One might be by means of a profound inner experience of God that was so deep, alive and intense that it burst out from within, giving physical evidence of the Stigmata on Francis' body. Another way presupposed a belief in angels. In Celano's account, he tells us that a seraph appeared and marked Francis. This was very unusual because seraphs were considered contemplatives and stayed hidden in heaven contemplating God. There was only one other instance in the history of salvation of a seraph coming to earth, which we find in Isaiah 6. Francis' account is the second instance. Lastly there is Bonaventure's account in the *Legenda Minor* XIII, which indicates that Christ appeared to Francis and affected the Stigmata.

La Verna is holy ground and is ours to walk on. The sanctuary is somewhat extensive. There are several chapels, the most important being the Stigmata Chapel, which guards the spot where Francis received the wounds of Christ. There is ample walking space along or up the mountain, rooms for staying overnight and a restaurant. On a visit there, remember to allow yourself to experience the mountain and tap into the spiritual energy that remains to this day.

Compassion
La Verna

The Little Flowers of St. Francis tell us that God wanted the mountain of La Verna to have a connection with Christ's Passion on Golgotha, "in order to show that the Passion of Christ was to be renewed on that mountain *in the soul of St. Francis by love and compassion* and in his body by the imprinting of the Stigmata."[1]

This statement invites us to explore how contemplation gives birth to compassion and love. It is something that is born of mystical experience and born of the cross. We can discover a pathway into this truth through an event that took place at La Verna. The Stigmata, no doubt, was an intense religious experience. Francis fasted and prayed for weeks, trembling before the face of God in which he questioned the journey of his life and his fidelity to the gospel. In the midst of this experience Francis saw the nail marks of Christ Crucified in his hands and feet. He had been changed into another man, into the image and likeness of the Crucified. Prior to this moment his companion, Leo, was separated from Francis by a deep chasm in the rock. Leo was in need, undergoing spiritual distress and anxiety. He wanted some written words from Francis for comfort that he could hold on to whenever he might doubt his vocation, but he was too timid to ask. Francis intuited his friend's need and made the effort to go to Leo. *The Second Consideration of Stigmata* puts it this way:

> [T]he Holy Spirit revealed to the Saint what Brother Leo did not tell him. St. Francis therefore called him and had him bring an inkhorn and pen and paper. And with his own hand he wrote a Praise of Christ, just as Leo had wished. And at the end he made the sign of the Tau and gave it to him, saying, "Take this paper, dear Brother, and keep it carefully until you die. May God bless you and protect you from all temptations!..."

Brother Leo accepted that writing with fervent love and faith. And at once all temptation left him.[2]

Franciscans today call this prayer *The Praises of God*. It came about as a heartfelt service to a brother in need. What was more reflective of Christ in Francis was not his Stigmata but this gesture of friend- ship and compassion. The transformation that occurred was not so much the marks of Christ's Passion appearing on his flesh as this deeper growth into compassion and tender gentleness.

One must feel Francis opening up now even more because of the cross, because of his mystical experience. This is what religious experience and gospel love do. It demands an immense price but reaches out. It does not close back in or keep the treasure for one- self. The price is not even noticed because the other is far more important. The focus is not on what has happened to me, or on wanting some extraordinary experience of God, but on others. Francis welcomed Leo. His share in the Passion made his sensitiv- ity more acute.

This leads us to understand that love is learned from God. John tells us that God is love, and love is of God. Love consists in that God has loved us. When we experience tenderness, gentleness, compas- sion, which we slowly become aware of in our growth with God, this disposes us to be gentle and compassionate in dealing with others and, of course, ourselves. When we embrace the cross and our own suffering, we come to be at peace and know a tenderness that comes from prayer.

Saint Paul speaks of learning how to love one's sister or brother warmly from encountering the divine warmth. He writes, "Blessed be the God and Father of our Lord Jesus Christ, the Father of mercies and the God of all consolation, who consoles us in all our affliction, so that we may be able to console those who are in any affliction with the consolation with which we ourselves are consoled by God" (2 Corinthians 1:3–4).

The compassion referred to here is of God. It is not our innate, native warmth. Good as our natural abilities may be, and useful as they are as a basis for what the Spirit brings, it remains unstable, dependent on the dispositions of a bestower and receiver. For us it is here one day, gone the next, shown to one person, not to another.

But a compassion, a warmth, a love born of contemplation, born of God, born of suffering, born of mystical experience is very different. Being rooted in a firm love of God, a love that cannot be substantially shaken by passing temptations or petty faults, a critical comment or a harsh word, it is a warm and stable love that varies little from day to day, consistent in its intensity and manifestation.

Note Francis' prayer at La Verna. He asked for two graces: pain and love. He was given both, one in his body marked by the wounds, the other in his heart by his gesture of compassion to Leo. He gave to Leo the compassion he received from God.

At times we would like to have something special happen to us in our relationship with God, perhaps like a stigmatic moment. And we can find ourselves disappointed, discouraged or just hurting because nothing is happening. There is no consolation. Perhaps, however, if we sense a deeper gentleness, more sensitivity, more respect and reverence for ourselves and others, a keener broadening of our spirit and a stretching of our minds, then maybe that something will have happened. This could be the stigmatic moment of our lives, the breakthrough of a deeper conversion taking place.

The sense of compassion and consolation first came through the Passion of Jesus. His response in obedience revealed the love of the Father for all. Through the Stigmata Francis entered more fully into this same mystery and power of healing compassion. He did this not only with Leo but throughout his life. His experience opened him to his brother, which also confirmed his Gospel life.

Our calling is similar. It is one of love and compassion, born of contemplation and the cross. Through this we enter more deeply into the love and gentleness of God. We learn how to love by experiencing God's love, which we then offer to all.

Here are *The Praises of God*, the prayer Francis composed at La Verna for Leo. It comes out of Francis' searing experience of God during September of 1224.

You are the holy Lord *Who does* wonderful things.
You are strong. *You are great.* You are the most high.
You are the almighty king. You *holy Father*,
King of *heaven and* earth.
You are three and one, the Lord *God of gods*;
You are the good, all good, the highest good,
Lord God *living and true*.
You are love, charity; You are wisdom, You are humility,
You are patience, You are beauty, You are meekness,
You are security, You are rest,
You are gladness and joy, You are our hope, You are justice,
You are moderation, You are all our riches to sufficiency.
You are beauty, You are meekness,
You are the protector, You are our custodian and defender,
You are strength, You are refreshment. You are our hope,
You are our faith, You are our charity,
You are all our sweetness, You are our eternal life:
Great and wonderful Lord, Almighty God, Merciful Savior.[3]

Canticle of the Creatures
San Damiano

Some of my clearest insights into Francis' *Canticle of the Creatures* developed from what I considered a personal flaw in my makeup. Until I was twenty-five years old, I never knew a day in my life that I did not stutter. I was going through the seminary at a time when we all took turns being first and second chanter for Divine Office, and reading meditation reflections in chapel, or reading Scripture in the dining room. Every time it was my turn, it was sheer terror. I knew what was coming and so did everyone else.

During my third year in theology I had a particularly difficult experience. I could not continue my turn, and afterward the director of students and the professors naturally questioned whether I should go on and be ordained to the priesthood. But from that point on I slowly began to accept myself. I did not realize it at the time, but I was accepting my poverty, my human condition, my creatureliness, my insecurity in speech. And I stopped stuttering, at least to a point. It still occurs now and then, but there is acceptance and I know inner peace.

I have experienced again and again how God's power works through such poverty, and through the freedom that comes from accepting the creature that I am. For my whole life has been that of public speaking: preaching, lecturing, leading prayer and the sacraments. I have experienced over and over how people's lives have been touched through this apparent helplessness in myself, and for this I will always be deeply grateful for Saint Paul's words in 2 Corinthians 12:7–10:

> Therefore, to keep me from being too elated, a thorn was given to me in the flesh, a messenger of Satan to torment me, to keep me from being too elated. Three times I appealed to the Lord about this, that it would leave me, but he said to me, "My grace is sufficient for you, for power is

made perfect in weakness." So, I will boast all the more gladly of my weaknesses, so that the power of Christ may dwell in me. Therefore I am content with weaknesses, insults, hardships, persecutions, and calamities for the sake of Christ; for whenever I am weak, then I am strong.

One time when I went through a hurting experience in my life I started stuttering again very badly and avoiding people. It is frightening when this happens. But peace came when I stopped blaming others for my run-down condition and accepted myself again, as I am, at a deeper level. I was accepting my poverty once more, my creatureliness, and would not allow it to cripple me.

Even now, each time I open my mouth to speak I am aware of the potential to stutter. It never leaves. The poverty, the creatureliness, is always there; it will not ever go away. I can only surrender to it, surrender to my being a creature, and accept. When I do, there is peace. I am no longer at war in myself. The battle is over.

There is probably no greater war human beings fight with themselves than the Creator-Creature conflict. It is very subtle. Each of us wants to be our own God, or a god unto ourselves—all powerful, in need of no one. These gods could be ambition, control, money, position, pride, a sense of superiority, food, alcohol or something like stuttering. Whatever it is, we have to deal with it in order to grow beyond it.

To the extent we resolve this conflict, we will have an understanding of the *Canticle of the Creatures*. It was Francis' grasp of his poverty, his creatureliness, that enabled him to compose and give meaning to the *Canticle*. This gave rise to two principal factors within Francis that lay at the foundation of his genius and insight regarding the *Canticle*, namely, Poverty and Sacramentality.

This singer of the *Canticle* recognized the sun and moon, earth and air, fire and water, all animals and plants, and death itself as brothers and sisters. This was grounded in one insight, namely, all creatures are *united in the depths of their being* by the fact of their being creatures, that is, by their creaturely poverty.

When Francis referred to Brother Wolf or Sister Water, he was not just using a clever metaphoric style. He meant those titles quite literally. The implications are rather extraordinary for one who takes this "brotherhood" and "sisterhood" seriously. What is the proper way to treat a brother or sister? Brothers and sisters are not to be exploited or manipulated, but rather they are loved and respected because of their family ties. To expand this concept to include everything that exists and to do it seriously leads to some rather startling behavior on Francis' part. In one instance, one of his garments caught on fire, but he refused to put it out because he did not want to harm Brother Fire. Similarly, we are told that Francis did not like to extinguish a candle or lamp. At times he would set loose fish that had been caught, would pick up worms off the road and seriously preach to flowers. These are some of Francis' "eccentricities" from a modern viewpoint. But what we really see here is a man who takes absolutely seriously his belief in the brotherhood and sisterhood of all creatures and the fatherhood of God and tries to act on that belief at all times. One is tempted to wonder whether Francis thought the flowers heard his sermons. That is not such a silly question as it is often made out to be. Obviously Francis realized that flowers could not hear. However, he believed that it is the nature of all things to praise their creator. Francis may not have had any idea how flowers or rocks would or could do this, but he acted on the belief that they could.

The basis for this approach to living is the discovery of one's finiteness, a recognition of one's poverty, one's creatureliness. If we can grasp the "iffiness" of existence and the sometimes shocking fact that the source and foundation of our being is not in ourselves, then we know ourselves as truly poor. To be poor in this fundamental sense is a definition, not a description. It defines who I am. This fundamental poverty makes me equal to all God's creatures. The human person has no more claim to intrinsic being than a plant or animal, a star or a stone. This is in no way to deny the unique role that the human person plays in the divine economy. Indeed, in light of the Christian doctrine of the Incarnation, that role is one of extraordinary dignity.

When all else has been said, the great truth that must be proclaimed is that we did not make ourselves. And so for Francis it was neither human self-denigration nor some poetic delight that led him to address the sun and the moon, the fire and the earth, and all animate and inanimate creatures as his brothers and sisters; it was the simple truth of shared creaturehood.

The other insight Francis offers for an understanding of the *Canticle* is that of sacramentality. The purpose of a sacrament is to reveal God's love and self gift. The Catholic tradition has recognized seven particular sacraments that manifest this truth, but every creature, human and nonhuman, animate and inanimate, can be a sacrament. Everything God created reveals something of God's goodness and love. Thus Francis of Assisi's interweaving of poverty with the brotherhood and sisterhood of all creatures is profoundly Catholic because it is profoundly sacramental. That is, creation points to, and reveals, God. Everything is a footprint of God.

Several stories from the early biographies make clear what separates Francis from others who were inspired only by a stunning sunset or lush meadows and rolling hills. In a leper Francis discovered the image of Christ because of the prophetic descriptions of

Christ in the Suffering Servant Song of Isaiah. When Francis saw two sticks crossed on the ground, they led him to meditate on Christ and his cross. One of Francis' greatest gifts to posterity was alerting Christians to the principle that God is manifest in each detail of the physical world to those who know how to "see" him. However, one does not see what is there if one does not look upon creation as a family. If we see nature only in terms of what it offers us (the number of kilowatt hours a dammed river could provide, the number of bushels of wheat an acre of land can produce or the economic feasibility of running day trips into the Grand Canyon), we will never find the traces of God there.

Francis of Assisi's love and praise of nature go far beyond the beautiful sunset and are more comprehensive than a modern environmentalist's concerns. The creatures are loved in themselves because they share their creaturehood with us and are therefore parts of our family, and for the way they can lead us to God.

Many picture Francis of Assisi as a romantic wandering through nature, speaking to birds and drawing the elements close to him. We might also have this image whenever we hear or pray the *Canticle*. In *The Assisi Compilation*, we find the context in which the *Canticle* was composed. The year was 1225. Francis was quite ill at the time and the Brothers took him to San Damiano where Clare and the Sisters could care for him.

> Blessed Francis lay there for more than fifty days, and was unable to bear the light of the sun during the day or the light of a fire at night....
>
> In addition, day and night he had great pains in his eyes so that at night he could scarcely rest or sleep....
>
> Sometimes he did want to rest and sleep, but there were many mice in the house and in the little cell made of mats

where he was lying.... They were running around him, and even over him, and would not let him sleep. They even disturbed him greatly at the time of prayer. They bothered him not only at night, but also during the day, even climbing up on his table when he was eating....

One night as blessed Francis was reflecting on all the troubles he was enduring, he was moved by pity for himself. "Lord," he said to himself, "make haste to help me in my illnesses, so that I may be able to bear them patiently." ...[During that night Francis was given the assurance of a great treasure awaiting him, together with much comfort and consolation.]

The next morning on rising, he said to his companions:..."Therefore for His [God's] praise, for our consolation and for the edification of our neighbor, I want to write a new Praise of the Lord for his creatures, which we use every day, and without which we cannot live...."

The Praises of the Lord that he composed...he called "The Canticle of Brother Sun," who is more beautiful than all other creatures and can be most closely compared to God.[1]

It would be helpful to read the whole of chapter 83 in The Assisi Compilation but the above passage gives us the context out of which the Canticle was born. Note that Francis was lying on the floor, sick, blind, in a hut made of reeds so as to shut out light and wind and be in darkness. When we consider that Francis could barely see, that fire, sun and light caused him severe head pains, that water made his wounds ache, that mice crawled all over him, that mother earth was not kind to his body. When we meditate on the fact that Francis was caught in self-pity, despair and pain, that he was experiencing severe doubt even at the end; when we consider all this and that the

Canticle was born from this setting, then we begin to wonder what the *Canticle* really means. Obviously, it was not the musings of a romanticist wandering among the beauties of creation, wholly taken up by what he saw. Some of the finest scholarship today invites us to discover that this *lauda* (hymn of praise) is a song whose theme is reconciliation. After being blessed with the assurance of heaven, Francis searched for someone, something to help him praise this Almighty God who had come to him in his profound need. He turned to the creatures around him, and in union with them, in reconciliation with them, with a heart that recognized that he and they, as creatures, were brothers and sisters under one Creator, lifted his voice in praise to his Lord. They would be his path of praise. It was a profound moment of reconciliation, and was perhaps the deepest moment in Francis' ongoing conversion.

The *Canticle* was written in three parts. The first was in the autumn of 1225 and began with the words "Most High" and ended with the words "flowers and herbs." In this section the dedication of praise to the Most High was followed by six strophes of alternates: brother sun - sister moon / brother wind - sister water / brother fire - sister earth. Brother-Sister alternated in pairs and spoke of bondedness and reconciliation. Paternity opened the poem: Brother Sun, male, dominating. Maternity closed the poem: Our Sister, Mother Earth, female who nourishes, feeds, produces. Between these two all others were reconciled.

Here is the text of the first part:

Most High, all-powerful, good Lord,
Yours are *the praises, the glory*, and *the honor*, and all *blessing*.
To you alone, Most High, do they belong,
 and no human is worthy to mention Your name.
Praised be You, my *Lord*, with all *Your creatures*,

especially Sir Brother Sun,

Who is the day and through whom You give us light.

And he is beautiful and radiant with great splendor;

and bears a likeness of You, Most High One.

Praised be You, my Lord, through Sister *Moon* and *the stars*,

in heaven You formed them clear and precious and beautiful.

Praised be You, my Lord, through Brother Wind,

and through the air, cloudy and serene, and every kind of weather,

through whom You give sustenance to Your creatures.

Praised be You, my Lord, through Sister *Water*,

who is very useful and humble and precious and chaste.

Praised be You, my Lord, through Brother *Fire*,

through whom *You light the night*,

and he is beautiful and playful and robust and strong.

Praised be You, my Lord, through our sister Mother *Earth*,

who sustains and governs us,

and who produces various *fruit* with colored flowers and herbs.

The second part was probably composed in July 1226. The bishop and the mayor of Assisi were embroiled in a scandalous feud. So Francis added two verses about forgiveness and sent two brothers to sing the song for the bishop and the mayor, which led to peace and reconciliation between them.

Praised be You, my Lord, through those who give pardon for Your love,

and bear infirmity and tribulation.

Blessed are those who endure in peace

for by You, Most High, they shall be crowned.

And finally on his deathbed in October 1226 Francis added the final verses as he welcomed Sister Death, reconciling his life with this sister.

> Praised be You, my Lord, through our Sister Bodily Death,
> from whom no one living can escape.
> Woe to those who die in mortal sin.
> Blessed are those whom death will find in Your most holy will,
> for *the second death* shall do them no harm.
> *Praise* and *bless* my *Lord* and give Him thanks
> and serve Him with great humility.[2]

It seems then that this *Canticle* is a poetic expression of reconciliation within the human person between the highest of his or her aspirations ("Most High"), and the deepest and most obscure attachments that he or she has with Mother Earth. There seems to be the meeting of the Most High in the depths of oneself while in communion with that which is most simple here. "The way of great humility" (end of the *Canticle*) and of "fraternal communion" with creatures becomes the way of total reconciliation of the soul with itself. Francis is an example of all this.

If in Assisi visit San Damiano and pray the *Canticle.* In doing so remember Francis, and perhaps hear a call to reconciliation, striving to break down all barriers among people everywhere, and between ourselves and the environment. All this happens only if we recognize, in our poverty, that there is one God alone, one Creator, and we, as God's creatures, are brothers and sisters to one another.[3]

Reconciliation
Santa Maria Maggiore

On a visit to the sanctuary of Santa Maria Maggiore in the lower part of Assisi, one comes to a courtyard entrance to the bishop's headquarters for the diocese of Assisi. Just before entering the driveway there are two images hanging on the walls. The one on the left portrays two brothers singing the *Canticle of Brother Sun*; the other on the right shows the mayor of the city kneeling at the feet of the bishop asking forgiveness, referred to in the previous chapter. They are a reminder of an event that took place here probably in late 1225. *The Assisi Compilation*, describes the scene:

> At that same time when he [Francis] lay sick, the bishop of the city of Assisi at the time excommunicated the podestà [mayor]. In return, the man who was then podestà was enraged, and had this proclamation announced, loud and clear, throughout the city of Assisi: no one was to sell or buy anything from the bishop, or to draw up any legal document with him. And so they thoroughly hated each other.
>
> And so, for that reason, [Francis] composed one verse for the *Praises:*
>
> Praised be You, my Lord, through those who pardon for Your love, and bear infirmity and tribulation.
>
> Blessed are those who endure in peace
>
> for by You, Most High, they shall be crowned.
>
> [Then Francis sent two of his brothers saying:] "Go and sing the *Canticle of Brother Sun* before the bishop, and the podestà"....
>
> When the *Praises of the Lord* were ended, the podestà...cast himself at the lord bishop's feet, telling him: "Look, I am ready to make amends to you for everything, as it

pleases you, for the love of our Lord Jesus Christ and of his servant, blessed Francis."

Taking him by the hands, the bishop stood up and said to him: "Because of my office humility is expected of me, but because I am naturally prone to anger, you must forgive me." And so, with great kindness and love they embraced and kissed each other.[1]

It is a tender story and a rare happening, but it prompts us to consider the importance and value of forgiveness. So often people are willing to forgive, but only on the condition they get every cent owed. Then others are willing to restore lost peace, but only if the other, especially the offending party, makes the first move. There are those who are willing to accept an offender, provided the person show proof of a change of attitude. We never hear phrases like "on condition that" or "only if" or "provided that" from Jesus.

Forgiveness is most difficult, especially if we have been hurt badly. But forgive, we must. Unless I am a forgiving person, I will not have the capacity for growth, for inner peace and freedom. I will not be able to pray. I will carry a closed and perhaps a miserable and bitter person wherever I go.

Henri Nouwen shares an insightful reflection:

There are two sides to forgiveness: giving and receiving. Although at first sight giving seems to be harder, it often appears that we are not able to offer forgiveness to others because we have not been able fully to receive it. Only as people who have accepted forgiveness can we find the inner freedom to give it. Why is receiving forgiveness so difficult? It is very hard to say: "Without your forgiveness I am still bound to what happened between us. Only you can set me free." That requires not only a confession that we have hurt somebody but also the humility to acknowledge our dependency on others. Only when we can receive forgiveness can we give it.[2]

Francis must have known this instinctively because as he brought together the mayor and bishop, the story clearly shows how both parties surrendered to the giving and receiving of forgiveness. Fear makes us want to run away from giving or receiving forgiveness. Maybe it is because we fear anger or rejection, or are afraid of being hurt again. These are reasonable fears, but they account for only one side of reality. Hidden in the heart of even the most hardened sinner is an untapped reservoir of goodness. That goodness can be drawn forth and helped to grow. But first it has to be seen, and named and hoped in. Francis intuited the goodness in both persons. His gesture freed them to see not only their own goodness, but also that of the other.

If we can forgive, which is always the last stage in a healing process, then gentleness and tenderness enter in. We understand more of God. We are healed and can bring healing to others. We grow on the inside. God needs a heart of flesh that becomes pliable in God's loving hands, often through the crucible of pain and hurt and suffering. It is a divine quality, something we are not able to do on our own power. Someone once wrote, "we are like beasts when we kill; we are like humans when we judge; but we are like God when we forgive." Forgiveness is the measure of our love for one another, a sign of our faith in Christ the Lord. Forgiveness brings the right kind of heart before God in prayer, and it is the reflection of our own experience of forgiveness from God.

Francis once wrote a letter to a minister (the person responsible for a fraternity) who wanted to be released from his position because it seemed he was being treated badly by some of the brothers. Francis encouraged him to love those who do such things, and not even wish that they be better Christians. He then added some tender and touching words:

> And if you have done this, I wish you to know in this way if you love the Lord and me, His servant and yours: that there is not any brother in the world who has sinned—however much he could have sinned—who, after he has looked into your eyes, would ever depart without your mercy, if he is looking for mercy. And if he were not looking for mercy, you would ask him if he wants mercy. And if he would sin a thousand times before your eyes, love him more than me so that you may draw him to the Lord; and always be merciful with brothers such as these.[3]

I think these words describe an attitude and characteristic of Francis that made him so appealing. Who would not be drawn to a man in whom they would find welcome and acceptance and forgiveness no matter what. If this stance were ours it could lead us, and others, into the kingdom.

Abundance From a Small Portion
La Foresta

La Foresta, one of four Franciscan sanctuaries in the Rieti Valley, is about three miles from the city of Rieti. It was the scene of a memorable event in the life of Saint Francis. His health was deteriorating rapidly, and so in the summer of 1225, in obedience to the wishes of Cardinal Hugolino, he agreed to set out for Rieti. The Cardinal had hope that the papal surgeon might be able to help Francis and alleviate his suffering.

News of Francis' arrival preceded him, and to escape the crowds, he detoured to San Fabiano at La Foresta and asked hospitality of the poor priest who ministered there. The people discovered where Francis was staying, followed him, and while there helped themselves to the grapes of the priest's vineyard. This would become the setting for the miracle of the grapes. *The Assisi Compilation*, describes the happening:

> That church had a small vineyard next to the house where blessed Francis was staying. There was one door to the house through which nearly all those who visited him passed into the vineyard....
>
> Some picked the grapes and ate them there, while others picked them and carried them off, and still others trampled them underfoot.
>
> The priest began to be offended and upset. "I lost my vintage for this year!" he said. "Even though it's small, I got enough wine from it to take care of my needs."
>
> When blessed Francis heard of this, he had him called and said to him: "Do not be disturbed or offended any longer....
>
> But, tell me, how many measures of wine did you get when your vineyard was at its best?"
>
> "Thirteen measures, father," the priest responded.

"...Trust the Lord and my words, and if you get less than twenty measures of wine, I will make it up to you."

The priest calmed down and kept quiet. And it happened by divine dispensation that he obtained twenty measures and no less, just as blessed Francis had told him.[1]

The wonder of this miracle has to do with an abundance coming from a little portion. Consider for a moment the gifts you have. They may be small; they may be great. If you keep them to yourself, they remain selfishly yours. If you share them, many others are enriched and inspired. Life expands abundantly.

One evening many years ago I had been in Assisi at Casa Papa Giovanni. A group of young students was there from northern Europe and had gathered in an upstairs garden. There was singing and the playing of musical instruments. At one point someone asked if anyone else present had a song to share. I sing very well and at the time played the guitar. But I was too shy and bashful to share my small gift, which I realized would have brought an abundance of joy and a connectedness to all present. Instead I trampled on my gift, kept it hidden and shared it with no one. I have never forgotten the episode because of the loss I felt.

Today La Foresta is a base for a Mondo X community, a program whose goal is to restore young people's lives that have been trampled down by various addictions. They enter the community with little hope for a future. They come from families and marriages that have disintegrated. Life is characterized by disorder, chaos and brokenness, with little or no self worth and surely no giftedness to offer others.

Through a unique program of honesty, trust, open communication, a daily assessment of life, bringing order back into nature and working with their hands, new life slowly emerges. From the dregs of a trampled down existence, self-confidence is reborn. Where there was nothing, the beginnings of "there's more to life" surfaces, and transformation takes shape.

Prior to the arrival of the Mondo X Community, the natural setting of La Foresta was in chaos. Little care had been given to the vineyards, flowers, a garden, creative artistic work and the natural beauty of the environment. With the establishment of the Mondo X program, order has returned, harmony is felt, creative energy can be felt, chaos is overthrown, and all has given rise to an abundance of newness and hope. Bringing order and harmony back into nature have been symbolic of bringing order and harmony back into the lives of the community.

For many La Foresta is a modern model of Francis' vision. It is a place where the Franciscan charism is lived out. Francis restored new and abundant life to everyone and in everything. He restored gospel life in the church and society. He gave a restored vision to nature through his *Canticle of the Creatures*. He restored life to outcasts and the poor who had been abandoned by all. Life in abundance burst forth because of him.

La Foresta today witnesses to that truth. La Foresta invites us to restore life wherever we are. La Foresta challenges us to believe abundance is within our reach, no matter how little or how much we have.

"I Have Done What Is Mine to Do"
Porziuncola

When the final days of Saint Francis of Assisi were drawing near, he returned to St. Mary of the Angels, the Porziuncola, where he had begun his gospel life. This place had always been most tender and special to him. It was here Francis wished to pass over into paradise.

There are accounts of various sayings of Francis as his final hours approached. One of the most significant is that provided by Thomas of Celano. He writes:

> As he was wasted by that grave illness which ended all his suf-ferings, he had himself placed naked on the naked ground, so that in that final hour, when the Enemy could still rage, he might wrestle naked with the naked. The fearless man awaited triumph and, with hands joined, held the *crown of justice*. Placed *on the ground* and stripped of his sackcloth garment, he *lifted* up his *face to heaven* as usual, and, totally *intent* upon that *glory*, he covered the wound on his right side with his left hand, so no one would see it. Then he said to his brothers: "I have done *what is mine; may Christ teach* you what is yours!"[1]

The key words are, "I have done *what is mine; may Christ teach* you what is yours." This is the legacy of Saint Francis.

Joseph Chinnici, O.F.M., has written an article entitled "The Spirit of St. Francis Today."[2] The gist of the article speaks of the need to allow the current myth of Francis to die. It has served its purpose. For example, we think of Francis as a person of exuberant joy, one who was happy and carefree. Are we not to imitate that spirit? Yet toward the end of his life he was quite angry with the brothers about the Rule. Then we have been given the impression that Francis was powerless, a minor. That certainly is true. But he was also well-connected with bishops and cardinals and Rome. On another level we can be led to believe that Francis was noble in dealing with women, beginning with Clare. Nonetheless he was a normal human being, an Italian man, full of passion. He had conflicting emotions and rolled in thorns and snow to deal with his temptations and lustful energy. And then there is the saga of Francis' absolute poverty. Francis, however, enjoyed benefits from the wealth of others and from a culture experiencing spurts of development and new freedoms. Francis had some fine pieces of real estate on which to pray and relax, Mount La Verna being one of them. And finally the myth of Francis' youthfulness and exuberance, being a troubadour for God, is held out to us. Yet Francis' life spoke most profoundly of God's love and his unity with him when the brothers were fighting and he was very ill. One has only to remember how the *Canticle of Brother Sun* came about.

The concern is that we are so preoccupied with keeping these images of Francis alive, and that somehow we are to be like him, that we do not allow the Spirit, which enlivened Francis, to enliven us. We nurture a myth (Francis was joyful, a troubadour, the poorest of the poor, always noble) to a point that it no longer relates to our experience and this prevents us from living with his spirit.

What should we do? Why not allow Francis to die and bury him once and for all so that our hearts can truly be open to the Spirit as was Francis'? We casually quote Francis when he said, "I have done *what is mine; may Christ teach* you what is yours." One might think Francis would advise his brothers and sisters, as he spoke his final words, to imitate him: Own nothing, be obedient, observe the Rule. Instead Francis affirms each person's unique response to God. He did not say "Imitate me!" but "Be open to Christ." This is what we need to understand and recapture in order to understand how to live a Franciscan vision of life in our time.

We commit ourselves to the gospel and a Franciscan vision of life as expressive of Jesus in our lives. But we also profess to grow. We commit ourselves to continue the ongoing development of our lives. We profess our ongoing openness to the Spirit who will guide and lead us and uncover new moments. In other words, we make a profession to Life, not to something dead, and claim with Francis: *"I have done what is mine; may Christ teach you...."*

One of our pilgrimage staff, Aaron Pembleton, was fond of saying to pilgrims, "Do you wake up each morning mired in mediocrity, or eager to face the new life and adventures of the day?" As if to say, "Oh God, another day! This job! These people! This spouse!" or, "Wow! I can't wait to get up, face the new challenges and discoveries of the day and take another step into the unfolding of the kingdom"? This is another way of saying, "May Christ teach me what is mine to do."

We need to let the myths of Francis die so that the Spirit that enlivened Francis and the first brothers can enliven us. What might happen if we do? Perhaps holiness of life will blossom—not some extraordinary or otherworldly kind of living, but a fully committed, dedication to our life and a fidelity to all that the gospel asks. Perhaps we will know a wholeness and freedom of Spirit inside, for the sake of the church, for the well-being of others and for our own happiness. Or perhaps we will discover the mystic within each of us. Who is the mystic? One who is overcome by God's love, God's Spirit, one who is drawn out of himself or herself in praise, gratitude, wonder and joy, one who truly has integrated Francis' words, *"I have done what is mine; may Christ teach you what is yours."* If we truly allow Christ to teach us what is ours to do, we could make a profound difference in society, family life and the church. Can this be possible? Without a doubt, because Christ has given us his Spirit to make it so. And his presence, his Spirit, abides with us always.

If you have an opportunity to visit St. Mary of the Angels in the valley below Assisi, there is a small chapel about twenty steps from the Porziuncola itself. It marks the spot where Francis died. Spend some time there and ask God to teach you what you are to do.

33

A New Kind of Fool
The Tomb of Saint Francis

The first time I knelt in the Crypt Chapel in the Basilica of St. Francis, I looked up at the Tomb of Saint Francis and said, "Francis, speak!" It was a plea that his spirit, encased in a stone sarcophagus, would break through, enter my spirit and transform my heart. In time I would learn that I was asking the impossible because only Jesus can transform my heart and renew my life.

Friar Christopher Coelho has written a book of reflections and music entitled *A New Kind of Fool*. He uses the title in reference to Francis who enjoyed being a *fool* for God. Francis accepted Christ and the gospel as completely as anyone ever could. For his time he truly was "a new kind of fool" for Christ. The question one might ask is what such a fool would look like, especially in our time. Scripture readings for celebrating the Feast of Saint Francis, something quite apropos when praying at his tomb, lead us toward some answers.

The first reading is from Sirach 50:1–4 and describes one who renovated the house of God in his time. He "fortified the temple," "laid strong foundations," "considered how to save the people from ruin," so that he appeared "like the morning star among the clouds," "like the sun shining on the temple of the Most High," and "like a rainbow gleaming in splendid clouds."

This fits Francis because in his time he renovated the house of God through his simplicity, humility and openness. Through him the Gospels were made new and visible. Living stones, alive with faith, were raised up. People were personally confronted with the realities of gospel life in the person of Francis. They were in the living presence of peace, forgiveness and compassion.

Such a person in today's language would be a refounding person, calling all to conversion by his or her life. A refounding person inspires a renewed vision of gospel life. Some might say,

"Franciscan life is useless, the church is out of touch, Christianity has no place in today's secular world. It's foolish to stay with it." A fool today takes up the gospel, takes it seriously and invites others to the same. The foolish one rebuilds, rebounds, calls others back to the gospel. The words from Sirach apply, "Behold him who in his life repaired the house...and fortified the temple."

Another Scripture text for the Feast of Saint Francis is from Galatians 6:14–18. Paul says, "May I never boast of anything except the cross of our Lord Jesus Christ, by which the world has been crucified to me, and I to the world.... I carry the marks of Jesus branded on my body."

A "fool for Christ," then, would be one who takes up the cross of Christ, finds purpose and meaning in the cross. This could imply obedient and full surrender to others. It is a love that gives them a right to make demands on us, to use us. Doesn't that sound foolish? Taking up the cross implies a willingness to suffer by being nonviolent. It implies an extravagant, generous, self-giving of one's life that does not count the cost. It is an extravagant opening of one's arms to embrace all, a self-giving that is patient, that seeks justice and one that resists the cycle of lashing back by imitating Christ.

When we read the Passion of Christ, the Gospel writer presents a model of nonviolent, passive resistance in the person of Jesus. When the Sanhedrin accused, when Pilate interrogated, when the soldiers crowned, struck, spat, when Jesus was being crucified, how did he respond? He opened his arms to a cross and on the cross. Jesus had no macho image to maintain, no political cause to defend, no high position to guard, no pride to protect. It was not his concern to be proved right, only to be true, and to maintain his integrity, to love to the end and show the world a way—the only way—to diffuse the violence in our nature.

All this appears foolish and stupid, and will always appear as such in the eyes of the world. Just think how you feel even in reading these words in Scripture, these words about the cross and this model of love. We dismiss them. "Nice," we say, "but it won't work today."

Yet one embraces this manner of life because Christ did it, whose greatest folly in human eyes was the cross. So a "fool for Christ" takes up the cross, like Jesus. Remember Paul's words, "May I never boast of anything except the cross of our Lord Jesus Christ."

The Gospel for the Feast of Saint Francis is from Matthew 11:25–30. Here we discover that a "Fool for Christ" is willing to convert to childlikeness in order to receive the revelation of God. Jesus said, "I thank you, Father, Lord of heaven and earth, because you have hidden these things from the wise and the intelligent and have revealed them to infants; yes, Father, for such was your gracious will."

Some say the genius of Francis was that as an adult he converted to childlikeness and took on all the simplicity and openness that this required. It meant being willing to receive, to let go and let oneself be ministered to, to leave roles behind and like a child welcome new discoveries. This is probably the most difficult kind of foolishness to submit to for in our adult sophistication we would say such thinking is demeaning. Yet in a unique way a child has the eyes and spirit to "see" and "receive" the revelation of God.

There is so much said about Francis of Assisi that one can easily focus too much on him. It is important to realize that the center of our attention is never on Francis but always on Jesus Christ and the gospel. Francis is like a finger pointing us to Christ. If we would, at this moment, find ourselves at the Tomb of Saint Francis, the setting would lend itself to such an axis point. Directly in front of us is the altar, the table of the Lord, which points us to Christ and all the mysteries of his life. If we did not know we were in the crypt chapel, the Tomb of Saint Francis would not be immediately noticed. It is nestled above the altar between two immense stone piers. It is not the first object that captures our attention. But therein lies the remains of the man we so admire, whose spirit attracts us, whose spirit leaps out from the stones encasing him and shows a way to live the gospel. Francis' spirit invites us to be a new kind of fool for Christ in our time.

34

New Generation in the
Franciscan Story
Basilica and Tomb of Saint Clare

As we examine the literature of Francis, we see that Clare is central to understanding the vision and mission of Francis. Francis hears from the crucifix at San Damiano, "Francis, go rebuild My house; as you see, it is all being destroyed." The one who fulfilled that mission at San Damiano was not Francis but Clare during the forty-one years she lived there. That is why it is important to come to know Clare, to move and breathe in her spirit. She carries out the mission of Francis; she lives out his vision perhaps more than any of the others, even among the first companions.

After Clare died in 1253, the basilica built in her honor was begun, being completed in 1260. This Basilica of St. Clare has great symbolic value for everyone because of its role as a place in the Franciscan story. It stands as a symbol of the new age in Franciscan life that began with Clare's death and burial. The first Franciscan woman, who encompassed Francis' vision for twenty-seven years after his death, is no longer. Thus a new chapter begins with this building.

Today we are the new generation, the current chapter in the unfolding of the Franciscan story. We are called to continue the work of rebuilding and renewing. It is no accident that the original crucifix of San Damiano hangs in the Basilica of St. Clare. As time and history run its course, this crucifix continues to be a source of inspiration and challenge for our lives. It is still perhaps the most effective rebuilding tool we have. Let it hang before us in our favorite place of prayer. As Francis and Clare drew inspiration from it, may the same be true for us. May we hear its message and allow its power to transform hearts so as to rebuild society, the church and our lives.

[NOTES]

Chapter 1

1. Regis J. Armstrong, O.F.M. CAP., J.A. Wayne Hellmann, O.F.M. CONV., William J. Short, O.F.M., eds. *Francis of Assisi, Volume II, The Founder. Early Documents* (New York: New City, 2000), p. 263.
2. Arnaldo Fortini, *Francis of Assisi: A Translation of Nova Vita di San Francesco by Helen Moak* (New York: Crossroads, 1992), p. 85.
3. See *Francis of Assisi, Volume II, The Founder,* p. 249.
4. Regis J. Armstrong, O.F.M. CAP., J.A. Wayne Hellmann, O.F.M. CONV., William J. Short, O.F.M., eds. *Francis of Assisi, Volume I, The Saint. Early Documents* (New York: New City, 1999), pp. 201–202.
5. *Francis of Assisi, Volume II, The Founder,* p. 542.
6. *Francis of Assisi, Volume I, The Saint,* p. 375.
7. *Francis of Assisi, Volume II, The Founder,* p. 634.
8. *Francis of Assisi, Volume II, The Founder* p. 387–388.
9. *Francis of Assisi, Volume II, The Founder,* p. 389.

Chapter 2

1. *Francis of Assisi, Volume II, The Founder,* p. 305.
2. *Francis of Assisi, Volume I, The Saint,* p. 133.
3. *Francis of Assisi, Volume I, The Saint,* p. 134.
4. *Francis of Assisi, Volume I, The Saint,* p. 102.

Chapter 3

1. *Francis of Assisi, Volume II, The Founder,* pp. 71–72.
2. Thaddée Matura, "Francis of Assisi: A Saint for Our Times," *The Cord,* 54.1, 2004, p. 35. Emphasis added.
3. Excerpts paraphrased from the *Testament, Francis of Assisi, Volume I, The Saint,* pp. 124–127.
4. *Francis of Assisi, Volume I, The Saint,* pp. 85–86.
5. Duane V. Lapsanski, *The First Franciscans and the Gospel* (Chicago: Franciscan Herald, 1976), p. 3.

Chapter 4

1. *Francis of Assisi, Volume II, The Founder,* p. 73.
2. *Francis of Assisi, Volume II, The Founder,* p. 247.
3. Regis J. Armstrong, O.F.M. CAP., J.A. Wayne Hellmann, O.F.M. CONV., William J. Short, O.F.M., eds. *Francis of Assisi, Volume III, The Prophet. Early Documents* (New York: New City, 2001), p. 588.
4. Constantines's Basilica of St. Peter, 4.

Chapter 5

1. *Francis of Assisi, Volume II, The Founder*, p. 73.
2. *Francis of Assisi, Volume II, The Founder*, p. 247.
3. *Francis of Assisi, Volume II, The Founder*, pp. 534–535.
4. William R. Cook, *Francis of Assisi, The Way of Poverty and Humility* (Wilmington, Del.: Michael Glazier, 1989), p. 35.

Chapter 6

1. *Francis of Assisi, Volume II, The Founder*, p. 249.
2. Clare, Second Letter to Agnes of Prague.
3. *Francis of Assisi, Volume I, The Saint*, pp. 283–284.

Chapter 7

1. *Francis of Assisi, Volume I, The Saint*, p. 244.
2. *Francis of Assisi, Volume II, The Founder*, p. 248.
3. Henri J.M. Nouwen, *Bread for the Journey* (New York: HarperCollins, 1997).
4. Nouwen, p. 56.

Chapter 8

1. *Francis of Assisi, Volume I, The Saint*, p. 124.
2. *Francis of Assisi, Volume II, The Founder*, p. 74.

Chapter 9

1. *Francis of Assisi, Volume II, The Founder*, p. 80.
2. Dennis Marie, Cynthia Moe-Lobeda, Joseph Nangle, Stuart Taylor. *St. Francis and the Foolishness of God* (Maryknoll, N.Y.: Orbis, 1993), p. 79.

Chapter 10

1. *Francis of Assisi, Volume I, The Saint*, pp. 201–202.
2. Lapsanski, p. 18.
3. *Francis of Assisi, Volume II, The Founder*, p. 86.
4. *Francis of Assisi, Volume II, The Founder*, p. 316.

Chapter 11

1. *Francis of Assisi, Volume II, The Founder*, p. 85.
2. *Francis of Assisi, Volume I, The Saint*, pp. 201–202.
3. *Francis of Assisi, Volume II, The Founder*, p. 85.
4. Nikos Kazantzakis, *Saint Francis* (New York: Simon & Schuster, 1962), p. 119.

5. Gerard Thomas Straub, *The Sun and Moon Over Assisi: A Personal Encounter With Francis and Clare* (Cincinnati: St. Anthony Messenger Press, 2000), pp. 21–23.
6. *Francis of Assisi, Volume II, The Founder*, p. 543.

Chapter 12
1. *Francis of Assisi, Volume II, The Founder*, pp. 85–86.
2. *Francis of Assisi, Volume II, The Founder*, p. 86.
3. Text courtesy of the Walters Art Museum.
4. Il messale consultato da S. Francesco, *San Francesco Patrono d'Italia* 58:82. Quoted in Fortini, p. 270.

Chapter 13
1. Lapsanski, p. 33.
2. Lapsanski, p. 56.
3. *Francis of Assisi, Volume II, The Founder*, p. 97.

Chapter 14
1. *Francis of Assisi, Volume I, The Saint*, p. 205.

Chapter 15
1. Adapted version from Joseph Wood, O.F.M. CONV., and Robert Melnick, O.F.M. CONV., *The Mirror of Perfection*, 27. Rivotorto, *The Protoconvento of the Friars Minor*.
2. *Francis of Assisi, Volume II, The Founder*, p. 99.

Chapter 16
1. *Francis of Assisi, Volume II, The Founder*, pp. 540–541.
2. *Francis of Assisi, Volume I, The Saint*, pp. 201–202.

Chapter 17
1. Ilia Delio, *Franciscan Prayer* (Cincinnati: St. Anthony Messenger Press, 2004), pp. 79–80.
2. *Francis of Assisi, Volume I, The Saint*, p. 133–134.
3. *Francis of Assisi, Volume I, The Saint*, p. 133.
4. *Francis of Assisi, Volume I, The Saint*, p. 135.
5. Delio, p. 83.

Chapter 18
1. *Francis of Assisi, Volume II, The Founder*, pp. 551–552.
2. *Francis of Assisi, Volume II, The Founder*, p. 314.

Chapter 19

1. Regis J. Armstrong, O.F.M. CAP., ed. *The Lady, Clare of Assisi. Early Documents* (New York: New City, 2006), p. 286.

Chapter 20

1. I am indebted to Ilia Delio for a penetrating exploration into Franciscan prayer during a course I attended at Washington Theological Union, Washington, D.C.
2. *The Lady, Clare of Assisi*, p. 42.
3. Delio, p. 128.

Chapter 21

1. *Francis of Assisi, Volume I, The Saint*, p. 201.
2. *Francis of Assisi, Volume II, The Founder*, p. 541.
3. *Francis of Assisi, Volume I, The Saint*, p. 49.
4. *Francis of Assisi, Volume II, The Founder*, pp. 291–292.

Chapter 22

1. *The Lady, Clare of Assisi*, p. 164.
2. *The Lady, Clare of Assisi*, p. 197.

Chapter 23

1. *Francis of Assisi, Volume III, The Prophet*, pp. 578–579.
2. St. Bonaventure, *On the Perfection of Life*, p. 6.

Chapter 24

1. *Francis of Assisi, Volume I, The Saint*, p. 207.
2. *Francis of Assisi, Volume I, The Saint*, p. 231.
3. *Francis of Assisi, Volume I, The Saint*, p. 74.
4. *Evangelization and Mission in the Order*, 1983.

Chapter 26

1. *Francis of Assisi, Volume I, The Saint*. pp. 254–255.
2. *Francis of Assisi, Volume II, The Founder*, p. 610.
3. *Francis of Assisi, Volume I, The Saint*, p. 256.

Chapter 27

1. Fortini, pp. 551–552.
2. Marion Habig, ed., *St. Francis of Assisi, Omnibus of Sources* (Chicago: Franciscan Herald, 1973), p. 1438.

Chapter 28

1. *Little Flowers of St. Francis.*
2. Habig, pp. 1438–1439.
3. *Francis of Assisi, Volume I, The Saint,* p. 109.

Chapter 29

1. *Francis of Assisi, Volume II, The Founder,* pp. 185–186.
2. *Francis of Assisi, Volume I, The Saint,* pp. 113–114.
3. Some of the ideas for this reflection are taken from Michael H. Himes and Kenneth R. Himes, "The Sacrament of Creation," *Commonweal,* 26 January 1990, pp. 42–49.

Chapter 30

1. *Francis of Assisi, Volume II, The Founder,* pp. 187–188.
2. Nouwen, p. 59.
3. *Francis of Assisi, Volume I, The Saint,* pp. 97–98.

Chapter 31

1. *Francis of Assisi, Volume II, The Founder,* p. 170.

Chapter 32

1. *Francis of Assisi, Volume II, The Founder,* p. 386.
2. Joseph Chinnici, O.F.M. "The Spirit of St. Francis Today," *The Cord,* Vol. 47, No. 2, March–April 1997, pp. 51–56.

[INDEX]

[SCRIPTURE INDEX]